Sinful **Sex**

Praise for Sinful Sex

'Accessible for both men and women . . . Loaded with info
that'll take you and your lover to nookie nirvana.'
Men's Health

'*Sinful Sex* has something for everyone.'
Daily Star

'Sizzling!'
The People

Sinful Sex

The Uninhibited Guide
to Erotic Pleasure

DR PAM SPURR

PORTICO

First published in Great Britain in 2002

This edition published in 2008 by
Portico
10 Southcombe Street
London
W14 0RA

An imprint of Anova Books Group Ltd

Reprinted in 2006, 2007, 2008

ISBN 9781861055460

A CIP catalogue record for this book is available from the British
Library.

 20 19 18 17 16 15 14 13 12 11

Printed and bound by CPI Mackays, Chatham, Kent, ME5 8TD

This book can be ordered direct from the publisher.
Contact the marketing department, but try your bookshop first.

www.anovabooks.com

Dedication

For anyone who's ever been disappointed with sex, I hope this guide helps you find more fulfilment. And for those who relish their sexuality, I hope this allows you even more erotic pleasures.

Contents

	Acknowledgements	ix
	Safer and Sinful Sex	xi
	Introduction	xiii
1	Sinful Self-pleasure	1
2	Sinful Stages of Sexual Pleasure	10
3	Sinful Sex Talk	26
4	Sinfully Unforgettable Foreplay	37
5	Sinful Positions & Places	56
6	Sinfully Delicious Oral Sex	86
7	More Sinful Suggestions	108
8	Sinful Fantasy Play	128
9	Sinful Toys, Playthings & 'Potions'	141
10	Sinful Sex Games & Scenarios	156
11	Sinful Solutions to Agony Questions	163
	Further Information	174
	The Seven Sexy Sins	176

Acknowledgements

I'd like to extend my sincerest thanks to those who've spoken so openly to me about their sex lives. Sometimes the path to enjoying our sexuality is a difficult one. Many of us can learn from those who've already made this journey and are prepared to share it.

My warmest thanks as always go to Jeremy Robson for his continued and valued support in my writing endeavours. Also to Joanne Brooks for her constructive ideas and sensitivity in editing. To my family, a heartfelt thanks for their never-ending patience. Last but not least, thanks to Kate Wood who probably never gets thanked enough!

Safer and Sinful Sex

Heed this warning now. You are responsible for your own sexual health and emotional wellbeing. I, as the author of *Sinful Sex*, cannot be held responsible for this aspect of your life. If you are with a lover whose sexual history you are not familiar with, you should practise safer sex at all times. This means during all penetration and oral sex techniques and any other situation where there is the possibility of exchanging bodily fluids.

The *proper* use of condoms (read the packet!) during both vaginal and anal penetrative sex is absolutely vital. It is also advised that condoms are used when performing oral sex on the male partner to serve as a barrier against the transmission of infections between mouth and penis. Equally, a barrier such as a dental dam (available from chemists) should be used when oral sex is given to a woman, vaginally or anally, and when a man receives oral stimulation of the anus ('rimming').

Some of the techniques in this book do not easily lend themselves to safer sex practices. Therefore they should only be tried with a partner you know and trust – and whose sexual history is fully known to you. Unfortunately, infidelity is widespread today so you should still exercise caution even if you are in a relationship.

Safer sex can be just as sinful and erotic as sex between two lovers who know each other's history and who do not use condoms/dams for protection against sexually transmitted diseases (STDs). The sensual, creative, and playful adorning of your partner's genitalia with condoms/dams/cling film (used carefully!) can be highly arousing. You can also use condoms or latex gloves on your fingers for manual stimulation of the genitals or anal area. Practice and imagination makes perfect!

Ideally, the very best way to ensure safer sex is to have a face-to-face consultation at your local surgery's family planning clinic, or at a well-man/well-woman clinic, where you will receive personal advice. You can also attend a GUM (Genito-Urinary Medicine) clinic for confidential advice. If you wish, you can remain anonymous. Alternatively, safer sex booklets are available at these clinics, most doctors' surgeries, bookshops and on Internet book sites.

Good luck – be sinful but be safer!

Introduction

Sinful beginnings

Do you crave deliciously sinful experiences and erotic pleasure? Do you want to, metaphorically, lap up every last drop of sensational sex with your lover? Then take this journey with me and allow yourself to develop every facet of your sexuality. You have everything you need within yourself to enjoy sinfully uninhibited sex – you simply may not have realised this potential.

Each one of you possesses your own unique sexuality that is there to be explored and enjoyed. I aim to provide you with the information and inspiration to get out and do it. The human sexual response is something truly exquisite and complex. It has the potential to give us ultimate pleasure, yet so many aspects of our lives stop us from fully enjoying our sexuality.

Unfortunately, many people find true sexual fulfilment is elusive. In fact many of you reading *Sinful Sex* will feel a little anxious about doing so. You may feel guilty, scared, or worried – emotions and attitudes that prevent you from truly relishing your sexuality. You may even be making lifestyle choices that prevent you from enjoying sex to the full – drinking or smoking too much, perhaps, or living with high levels of stress, or staying in unhappy relationships.

Another consideration is the complaint some people make that there's 'sex everywhere' – they feel that they can't escape it. But just because advertisers, television programmes, movies, magazines and so on, choose to exploit sex in various ways doesn't mean that all of us are living their commercial dream. On the contrary, it puts many of us under pressure to do 'it' like *everyone else* – instead of finding the sinful pleasures that do it *for us!*

Many of you, however, will be comfortable with your sexuality and are simply seeking some new techniques and ideas to bring to your lovemaking. The best lovers realise that they don't know it all – that there's always something more to learn. And that truly sinful sex is dynamic – it changes with the mood and the moment. Never believe lovers who claim to know everything and to be able to pleasure anyone. They probably only understand their own needs and then don't even realise how those can change and alter with circumstances.

I hope *Sinful Sex* will open your eyes to taking pleasure in your sexuality and introduce you to a new freedom to explore your own body and relish sex with your lover.

The most deliciously sinful sex is between consenting adults who are in control of their sexuality. This takes what I call the three 'Cs' of attaining and enjoying sex: *sexual confidence, communication* and *creativity*. These three areas are crucial to the development of your sexual pleasure and will be laced throughout this book.

And why have I called it *Sinful Sex*? Because I want you to be adventurous, to do something different, fresh and risqué. I'd like you to feel exquisite erotic pleasure, leaving behind your inhibitions, enjoying every little corner of your body, and revelling in the power of the emotions behind your sexual feelings, fully aware of the connection between mind and body. Before we get to truly sinful pleasure, I'd like to take you through self-pleasure – getting to know your own body – and the stages of sexual pleasure. Understanding these will prepare you for a fulfilling (and sinful!) sex life.

Many of the techniques and suggestions found in *Sinful Sex* can be applied to men and women. Often, the descriptions relate to one sex only, but this is purely to avoid repetition. In most cases, your partner will be able to practise the technique on you and you will be able to treat him or her with it too!

1

Sinful Self-pleasure

This chapter is crucial! You may be surprised to find a whole chapter devoted to this topic. In fact, it might be said that I'm on a bit of a mission to get people indulging in self-pleasure. The reason? You can't possibly achieve a sinful sex life without truly knowing your own sexual responses. Such sexual self-knowledge is absolutely imperative for deriving real pleasure. I can't stress this enough. This is where many other mediums of sex advice fall down – they simply don't emphasise how the basis of your sexual enjoyment largely rests with your ability to understand your own body.

I know this to be true from the thousands of people I have spoken to in my roles as agony aunt, life coach and psychologist. It is particularly true for females, as those women who really know their bodies tend to have more satisfying sexual relationships. Generally speaking, men are more willing to own up to masturbating. The famous American sex researcher Alfred Kinsey allegedly said that 98 per cent of men in his studies reported masturbating – and the other 2 per cent had lied!

However men, too, could get more out of their 'solo' experiences rather than simply experiencing brisk and basic sexual relief. For starters, they can use masturbation to help learn more control over their ejaculatory response – something most women would love them to do!

How does self-pleasure relate to mutual pleasure with your lover? I've heard many tales of people feeling 'lost in the dark' with their lovers and not having particularly good sexual relationships. In the next breath, they say how they shy away from enjoying their *own* sexuality. So I only have to put two and two together – and it doesn't add up to two cosy lovers!

The irony of this is that people expect to explore their lover's sexual response – but not their own! Why should theirs be any different? They should be exploring the fluid and dynamic qualities of their own sensuality; the many things that affect sexual feelings, not only from relationship to relationship but from day to day!

How can you possibly expect a lover to explore and pleasure you, if you can't do the same to yourself? If you find your own body so daunting, scary even, or a turn-off, or you're anxious about touching yourself, you'll transmit this anxiety in subtle ways (and maybe not so subtle ways) to your partner. If touching yourself seems so unpleasant or 'wrong' you'll find it hard to cross this negative emotional barrier and express to your lover what might feel good – fantastic even! You need to develop a positive sexual relationship with yourself before you'll truly enjoy sinful sex with your lover. This is analogous to what relationship experts mean when they say that until we learn to love ourselves we can't truly love another.

In other words, sex and love are two-way streets. As well as focussing on your lover's needs, you need to be able to express your own. Sexual communication will be covered in Chapter Two. The starting point here is *knowing* your sensual self. It's amazing how Victorian views on sex – and particularly their anxiety-raising convictions that masturbation caused anything from sterility to madness – still seem to lurk behind our modern-day feelings of sexual guilt. Well, we know that we're not going to go sterile if we pleasure ourselves – but does it make us perverts to masturbate, we wonder? Time to throw away any notions your parents (or possibly some of your past lovers) have given you that masturbation is sad, bad or dirty.

Getting sexy with yourself

I mentioned *sexual confidence* in the Introduction. Sexual confidence begins with self-knowledge. In most cases, the people I meet have low sexual confidence because they have low self-knowledge. Remember this simple equation: Self-knowledge = sexual confidence = self-pleasure = shared pleasure!

What is the best way to begin this fascinating journey into the way your sexuality expresses itself? The perfect starting point is to introduce you to the intricacies of the male and female genitalia and erogenous zones, with the help of some simple drawings. This will benefit those of you who don't realise all the many different *pleasure points* that await you. And for those of you who feel you *know it all*, simply treat this section as a refresher course!

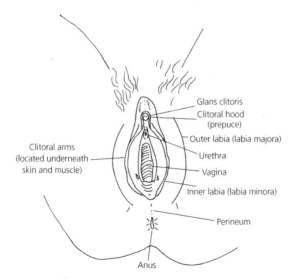

Please note: women's genitals come in all shapes and sizes. In 50 per cent of women, the inner labia protrude past the outer labia.

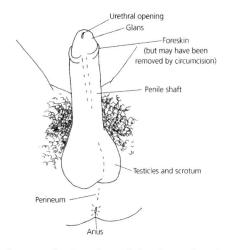

Urethral opening
Glans
Foreskin
(but may have been
removed by circumcision)
Penile shaft
Testicles and scrotum
Perineum
Anus

The art of masturbation doesn't begin and end with your genitals, however. So let me take you on a little journey around your main erogenous zones in the following illustrations. We don't want to leave any stone unturned in terms of erotic self-discovery! You may wonder why I refer to it as the 'art' of masturbation. Quite simply, masturbation ranges from the fast and furious self-administered 'quickie' to a luxuriant and leisurely, tender and slow, self-seduction. It can truly be an art to understand how your body responds. As you come to know your body – and how your moods and feelings affect its responses to stimulation – you can then treasure the richness of your sexual responses.

A sinful selection of your erogenous zones
From your scalp down to the tips of your toes, your body has a wealth of erogenous zones. Each person responds differently, though, and that's what makes every lover unique! What turns one person on, say, gentle stroking behind the knees, will feel awful, ticklish or overly sensitive to another. So let me show you around the body and, hopefully, this will help you to be more creative when you masturbate. You can then carry this delicious knowledge into your lovemaking.

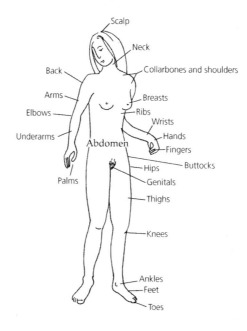

Scalp
Neck
Collarbones and shoulders
Back
Arms
Breasts
Elbows
Ribs
Wrists
Underarms
Hands
Abdomen
Fingers
Buttocks
Hips
Palms
Genitals
Thighs
Knees
Ankles
Feet
Toes

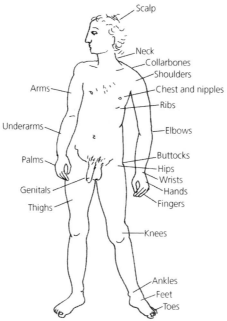

Scalp
Neck
Collarbones
Shoulders
Arms
Chest and nipples
Ribs
Underarms
Elbows
Palms
Buttocks
Hips
Wrists
Genitals
Hands
Thighs
Fingers
Knees
Ankles
Feet
Toes

Where you feel most comfortable
You need to learn to treasure yourself. And that means beginning where you're most comfortable. Ensure you are warm and relaxed. Most people will probably choose their bedroom. But once you've discovered the joys of self-pleasure, you might want to try somewhere new from time to time – the bath, shower, sofa, easy chair, and so on. And for something a bit more sinful – sitting in your office desk chair (behind locked doors!). Before you masturbate, you may want to use a visualisation technique (such as the one I describe below) to help you to relax. Or you could simply allow erotic thoughts and fantasies to wander slowly through your mind.

The type of touch
Now what do you do to all these lovely erogenous zones when you're going solo? Caress, scratch, tickle, massage, pinch and tap them with your fingertips, hands and wrists. You may find it more arousing to stimulate yourself with some sort of implement. For example, you could try gently massaging yourself with a vibrator or dildo (see page 143). Many women have confided in me that they masturbate using a silky scarf, which they gently pull back and forth over their clitoral region. You may choose to wear silky underwear for a supersensual feeling. You may find you get more pleasure by placing a pillow between your thighs, which you gently rub against. This is particularly effective for women who are very sensitive to direct stimulation or touch. Or you could use the palm of your hand. If you experiment by touching yourself in different ways, it will help you to discover how you want your partner to touch you and, in turn, enable you to be more imaginative when touching your lover.

 Sinful Secret . . . rather than use their hand, some women prefer to masturbate against something soft, such as a pillow.

It's important that you free yourself to touch your body how you want. There is no 'right' or 'wrong' way to masturbate. If you've never masturbated before, begin by lying back on your bed or in a warm bath and touching your upper body. Caress your breasts/chest and then gently pinch or stroke your nipples. Or you could allow your fingertips to run slowly across your neckline and then trace a path down your stomach to your lower abdomen. There you can begin to tease yourself. Pull slowly at your pubic hair or drum your fingertips back and forth over your pubic bone – using a light touch as if playing the most delicate of sonatas on a piano. Such gentle tapping sends arousing sensations across your genitals. It's up to you to decide when it's time to touch and stimulate your genitals. If you're in the bath or shower, you could tease yourself with the showerhead – enjoy the trickling of the water, slowly increasing the pressure to a point that feels fantastic to you. If you're a woman, remember always to point the showerhead downwards from the pubic bone and not up into the vagina, as there is a very small risk that you might force an air bubble into your bloodstream.

Sinful Secret... I highly recommend that a woman gets a hand-held mirror and examines all the lovely parts of her genitals. Many women have bizarre notions that their labia, clitoris and vagina are ugly. Instead, imagine them to be the parts of a rare and exotic flower that you are going to treasure.

Once you're building your pleasure and sexual tension towards orgasm you need to explore different ways of touching yourself in order to find what brings you to orgasm. You may need a rhythmic touch, a more pulsating touch, a brushing or pulling motion, and so on. It's the sensation you *love* that counts!

Sinful Secret... Breaking down inhibitions about masturbation is like breaking a bad habit, because your inhibitions are quite simply that — a 'habit' of thinking masturbation is 'wrong' or 'dirty'. And we all know that bad habits can be broken with a little effort!

Self-pleasure visualisation

Every day, set aside a few moments for yourself. Get comfortable and visualise yourself in your own soft, warm, self-contained place. 'Self-contained' is the crucial part. Place the visualisation anywhere you feel good – you could imagine lying on a lace-covered four-poster bed, or even on a small desert island. This is your private place where no one can intrude. Allow your mind to wander over it. Feel the safety it provides. No one can bother you. Now allow yourself to believe that your self-pleasure is part of this. You are allowed private moments to explore your unique sexual response in your safe and secret place.

Next, think through whatever negative thoughts you can identify (bad and habitual thinking prevents you enjoying self-pleasure). Does a parent's voice pop into your mind saying, 'Don't touch yourself – that's dirty!'? Perhaps you can't identify anyone specifically who gave you this negative and inhibiting message but simply hear this negativity bouncing around in your mind. It's time to relegate negative thoughts to a distant place, well away from the private pleasure haven you've visualised (desert island, four-poster, whatever). Imagine these thoughts in your mind – roll them up into a ball and toss them from your haven! The more you can believe you are in control of your sexual thoughts – the more you free yourself from negative messages from the past that influence your sexuality in the *present*!

Understanding orgasm

Masturbation is NOT just about reaching an orgasm. It's about you, your feelings, your fantasies, knowing your body and more. However, learning how to orgasm through self-pleasure is important, especially as you can then share this knowledge with your lover. This is better than joining the huge number of women (and some men) who can't orgasm with their sexual partner during penetrative sex or, in some cases, any kind of sex. So I bet you'd like to know a little about your orgasms! The next chapter will take you through the sensual processes that culminate in orgasm, making sex a sinfully special experience.

When masturbation is a problem
It is rare for masturbation to become a problem. However, like any form of behaviour, on rare occasions it can become compulsive. This is more common in men than women and has little to do with sex. Instead when a man starts to mastur-bate compulsively, it's often due more to stress and anxiety than anything else. It becomes a behaviour that provides a person with relief from certain negative mental states.

Compulsive masturbation disrupts the normal flow of life. Rather than choosing to indulge in some self-pleasure in a private moment, they feel compelled to do so. Such behaviour may interfere with a person's life and relation-ships, and usually requires professional treatment. But by far the majority of the population will find masturbation is a healthy pursuit with many benefits.

This is a good point to end this chapter. I hope you now feel willing, ready, and able to bring yourself to sinful self-pleasure! So relax and enjoy the private world of your sexuality. Chapter Two will give you a deeper under-standing of your sexual responses, preparing you to share this knowledge with a lover. You'll then be in the right sexual and emotional place to listen to and understand your partner's unique needs and sexual responses.

 Sinful Suggestion… Take a voyage of self-discovery tonight. Light a couple of candles in the bathroom, sprinkle your bath with a bath oil that smells and feels sensual, put on some soothing music, and give yourself permission to enjoy your own sexual responses. As the saying goes — 'you're worth it!'

2

Sinful Stages of Sexual Pleasure

Now is the time to delve into your own unique sexual responsiveness leading up to orgasm. As this is not a medical textbook, but a book designed to enhance your sinful pleasure, I'm not going to go into too much detail about the physiology of sexual response and orgasm, or problems relating to orgasm. Instead, I'd like to describe to you the basics of sexual pleasure that I have found to be important to the people I have spoken to in my years as a psychologist, agony aunt and writer.

Understanding the sexual stages
Let's begin with the build-up to orgasm. A person doesn't simply go from zero to full-on sexual arousal and orgasm in 0 to 60 seconds like a sports car! No, we are subtle creatures. Our bodies and minds go through a number of stages including desire, arousal, orgasm and, finally, resolution. For a man, on average, it is a case of 0 to approximately 11 minutes to build up to orgasm, and for a woman much longer – 0 to 28 minutes, on average. However, times vary tremendously. For example, a highly orgasmic woman may climax very quickly whereas some men can take longer to reach climax than their female

partners. This is an important point to learn, both in understanding your own sexual responses and sharing this information with your lover.

Sex researchers differ slightly in how they conceptualise the stages of pleasure from first arousal through to orgasm and beyond. For the sake of clarity, I'll run through all the stages suggested by different writers.

Stage one – drive
Sex drive varies enormously, ranging from those who totally lack any sort of drive to people with a very high libido. Of course, your sex drive is essential to how you see yourself as a sexual person. At one extreme, you may consider yourself highly sexed. At the other, you may feel 'indifferent' to sex. And there is any number of variations in between. As with all aspects of your sexuality, sex drive is affected by everything from your personal attitudes and beliefs to the side effects of some medications. If you have a low sex drive, the next couple of stages might be met with frustration. You may also have a problem if you have a very high level of drive and your lover doesn't.

Stage two – desire
Ninety-nine per cent of the time, sexual desire begins in your mind. You've undoubtedly heard it before but your mind *is* your most important sex organ – believe it! If your mind isn't there your body won't follow. You may have bags of sex drive but if you have no desire for the one you are in bed with – in other words, that person doesn't 'do it' for you – sex may not be on the cards. On the other hand, some people have the ability to think about something as mundane as stocks and shares and yet still go through the motions of full sex. That's fairly demoralising for their sexual partners, when you think about it!

In the main, it is the way you feel and think that dictates your sexual responsiveness. To initiate sexual desire, your mind must be involved. For example, *seeing* something that interests you at a sexual level – perhaps simply getting a loving gaze from your partner – can put thoughts of a sexual encounter into your mind. You may *hear* something that excites you – perhaps you're lying in bed in the early morning and your lover sighs and starts breathing deeply. This may remind you of the sounds your partner makes during sex – thereby getting your mind moving along an erotic pathway. A simple *touch* can stimulate desire. Your partner bends to kiss you goodnight and gently strokes your lower back at the same time – and your mind wanders off to the possibility of yet more enjoyment to come.

From these examples you can see that if your mind is elsewhere – dealing with work worries, financial trouble, stressful thoughts about your relationship – it'll be more difficult to switch over to sensual thoughts and sexual desire. If you don't feel any sexual desire, getting to the next stage is going to be difficult.

Stage three – arousal

Put simply, this is where your body catches up with your mind. Your erogenous zones start to spring to life (for example, your nipples become erect), your genitalia start to engorge with blood (this occurs in both women and men), and in women the process of natural lubrication usually begins within twenty seconds. Your breathing gets shallower, your muscles tense with anticipation – you show the physical signs of feeling sexy, horny, or randy – whatever you wish to call it. To illustrate the complexities of the arousal stage, let me describe two main scenarios.

Firstly, let's consider the emotional side of things and how this affects arousal. You may feel desire for your partner but if you also feel emotionally inhibited (perhaps you've got a negative 'voice' in your mind that says, 'sex is dirty') this may prevent your body *responding* to your sexual thoughts. One typical way this presents itself is when a woman does not produce enough natural lubrication before sexual activity – making sexual intercourse unpleasant, even painful. So, even though she has *desire* for her partner at one level, she doesn't progress into the physical stage of *arousal* (or she may partially progress with some signs of arousal) because of her inhibitions about sex.

Lubrication difficulties may also occur for other reasons, of course, perhaps as a result of the hormonal changes that women go through when they reach the menopause. This problem is often amenable to hormone treatment or more simply by introducing an over-the-counter lubricant to love-making.

Secondly, the arousal stage may be influenced by physical problems. For example, a man may *desire* his partner but be unable to become fully aroused, perhaps owing to circulatory problems (especially if he drinks and smokes heavily), or other medical disorders, or as a side effect of the medication he's taking. This is why it's important that anyone experiencing difficulties at any stage – desire, arousal or orgasm – discusses the matter thoroughly with their doctor.

 Sinful Secret . . . There are many things that can affect your sexual response including medication (even simple painkillers), smoking, too much caffeine, alcohol, a large meal, stress, anger and sadness.

Stage four – orgasm
Once aroused, people reach orgasm at very different rates. Women in particular can experience an extended *plateau* phase where they are highly aroused but need time to reach orgasm. In fact, many men (and their partners) wish they could extend their own plateau phase to allow time for their partners to catch up. In other words, their aim is to control and lengthen their arousal stage (in addition to the desire stage) to something approaching their partner's average of 28 minutes from start to finish!

The experience of orgasm varies tremendously between individuals but somehow we've all ended up under enormous pressure to 'get there'. It's become our modern goal – the way we measure ourselves as lovers. Do we have orgasms or not? If we do – what is their 'quality' and how many do we have? In other words, are we multi-orgasmic? If we don't have an orgasm then what's wrong with us? Considering that an orgasm only lasts under ten seconds in most cases, and rarely longer than twenty seconds, this emphasis seems strange.

Taking a historical perspective, when looking at that most famous of 'sex guides', the *Kama Sutra*, probably dating from the first century AD, the emphasis was far more on the spiritual side of lovemaking. Lovers were encouraged to meld the body and spirit together through the sexual experience. These teachings emphasised the path 'travelled' with your lover to reach orgasm – and not necessarily the orgasm itself. We can learn from these ancient principles.

Regarding your own sexual responses, I'd really like you to take the emphasis *off* reaching orgasm. There are two main reasons for this. First, once you learn not to concentrate on the very last few moments of your sexual enjoyment you may well find that you reach orgasm more easily. Second, even if you don't have any difficulty reaching orgasm, I believe this narrow focus detracts from simply enjoying leisurely foreplay and exploring different aspects of your, and your lover's, sexual responses.

Stage five – satisfaction and resolution
Some experts say that the final stage is orgasm, but others believe that following orgasm there is satisfaction and then *resolution* – involving a return to your normal physical state. During this stage, blood leaves the genitals, with the penis returning to its flaccid state, the muscles relax, and vaginal lubrication ceases. For men, this period lasts about twenty minutes on average. During this stage, also known as the refractory period (where his sexual apparatus 'resets' itself) he is unable to become aroused again. The refractory period increases with age. Young men may be able to get aroused again in only a few minutes, whereas for older men it may take an hour or more. For many women, the refractory period is often very short and they may be able to reach

arousal again quickly – especially if her lover sinfully stimulates her in the right way!

Female orgasm
There are important points to make about the differences between the female and male orgasm. First, more women than men report difficulties achieving an orgasm. Granted many men (roughly 40 per cent) may experience problems such as erectile difficulties at some point in their lives. However, most will reach orgasm through sex with their partners as well as through masturbation. So what are the female sex facts?

Research shows that about 40 per cent of women have difficulties at the desire and arousal phases – making reaching orgasm and satisfaction difficult. Studies vary, but around 25–33 per cent of women reach orgasm regularly during penetrative sex. About 13 per cent of women claim they always orgasm during sex. This contrasts with the 60 per cent or so who have great difficulty reaching orgasm during penetration. Furthermore, 10–15 per cent of women claim they never orgasm – a condition called anorgasmia.

With the right stimulation, the majority of women could reach orgasm during sex, as actual medical problems that impair the ability to orgasm are rare – and usually treatable. However, owing to poor communication (covered in the next chapter), inhibitions, lifestyle issues such as stress, or even the selfishness of some partners, many women's physical needs are not being met.

Sinful Fact... A very positive finding is that many couples now know that women orgasm more easily during oral sex and about 70 per cent of couples practise this — compared to a scant 20 to 25 per cent a couple of decades ago. So the message is getting across — it's all right to orgasm in any way you can — whether orally, manually, or a combination of these with intercourse.

Orgasm can be evaluated both subjectively (considering a woman's feelings about the experience) and physically through various measures used in sex research. Most women report reaching a 'peak' that may build gently and gradually, or come on quite quickly and 'violently'. Orgasmic sensations may include a strong feeling of rhythmic waves convulsing through her genitals and other regions. A woman will often experience different sensations during her various orgasmic experiences – sometimes weaker or gentler, other times stronger and literally able to take her breath away.

At the physical level, sex research has found a woman's body goes through many changes during orgasm. Briefly, these include rhythmic contractions of the vagina, the uterus and the anal sphincter. Women may experience muscle 'spasms' in the lower abdomen and buttocks, facial grimaces and a sense of a loss of time. Except for those rare women who practise *Tantric* sex and can achieve orgasm without direct clitoral stimulation, females need constant clitoral stimulation – of some sort. I'll repeat that – *of some sort!* The 'sort' is determined by each woman's special preferences for touch – right up to and through the point of orgasm.

The form that clitoral stimulation may take will vary from woman to woman (and may vary from day to day in the same woman!). Some women need *direct* clitoral stimulation to bring on an orgasm. Other women would jump out of their skin if someone touched their clitoris directly, and need more general stimulation across the pubic region in order to stimulate the clitoris *indirectly*. Some women need stimulation down the sides of the clitoris – the *clitoral arms*. It has only recently been discovered that the clitoral region extends much farther under the skin than just the clitoral bud and its immediate area. This is why sinful self-pleasure is so important. Once a woman learns exactly what form of stimulation will bring her to orgasm, she can share this knowledge with her partner.

Men and women differ greatly in this regard. A man may stop being physically stimulated, or the stimulation may change, but if he's reached his 'point of no return' he'll still ejaculate and experience orgasm. Even if stimulation stops just *before* this point of no return, he can quickly regain ground. For a woman, however, if stimulation stops – even just before orgasm – so too does her ability to climax. This is very frustrating for most women and it is often at this point, when they've lost the correct stimulation, that they decide to fake orgasm. In fact, approximately 95 per cent of women admit to faking an orgasm at some stage during sex, compared to just 30 per cent of men.

The fact that some men fake orgasm may be a surprise to you, and you may wonder how and why they do it. Well, they fake orgasm for many of the same reasons that women do. Because they sense, for whatever reason, that they're losing their erection, or are too tired to keep trying, and want to spare their partner's feelings. Men can make noises and movements as if they've reached orgasm just as easily as women! As there's generally quite a bit of lubrication during penetration (and if the man is wearing a condom and quickly takes it off, his partner will have no idea whether he's ejaculated into it or not), many women simply can't tell.

Sinful Secret… There is never a good reason to fake orgasm. It creates more problems than it solves! So, be honest and if you two are focussed on your general lovemaking (taking the emphasis off orgasm, as I've suggested) then this honesty shouldn't hurt either of you.

A minority of women may orgasm simply from vaginal and/or cervical stimulation (a few women claim that deep thrusting against their cervix brings on an orgasm). However, this may be due to the way the various nerves and tissues located within and around the vagina and clitoris are interconnected (as well as a subtle stimulation of the clitoral area, which the women may not have noticed) and how women perceive the various sensations involved in orgasm. Even this doesn't compare with some highly sensitive women who claim to be able to orgasm through stimulation of their breasts alone!

Other women claim 'G-spot' stimulation gives them the best possible orgasm. For many years, sex researchers have debated the existence of the G-spot – named after Ernst Gräfenberg, the German doctor who identified it in 1950. Debate has centred on two issues: does it exist at all? If it does exist, where is it exactly? Simply from the number of women who've told me they've located such a pleasure zone, I agree with the experts who believe it is a coin-sized, spongy mass of tissue located on the front, inner wall of the vagina, a few centimetres (about an inch or so) inside.

Some women (and their partners) find that stimulation of this area gives a novel sensation. According to some evolutionary biologists, this may be because sexual intercourse originally took place through rear entry (the man behind the woman, either standing or 'doggy' style). In order for the woman to be more receptive to intercourse, the G-spot was located where it could be optimally stimulated by rear entry.

When frontal entry became the norm, the clitoris would have been brought to life with stimulation during face-to-face intercourse. (As I'm a believer in the G-spot, I'll be covering G-spot pleasure in delicious detail in Chapter Seven!)

Another aspect of female orgasm that has sparked much debate is whether or not female ejaculation exists. More and more sex researchers now believe that up to 70 per cent of women ejaculate during the contractions of orgasm. The fluid is not urine – an idea that embarrasses many women – but it is also unlike regular vaginal lubrication. Some have suggested that female ejaculate is not unlike male prostate gland fluid. Putting the debate aside, unless a woman does have a problem with incontinence there should be no concern if she ejaculates with orgasm. Most importantly, women should enjoy all their unique responses to sexual stimulation.

 Sinful Secret . . . Forget an 'apple a day keeps the doctor away' – an orgasm a day will achieve this as it boosts the body's levels of certain endorphins (naturally occurring mood enhancers), in turn boosting the number of lymphocytes – important for your immune system!

Male orgasm

A man's orgasm occurs in two phases, during which he undergoes distinct physical changes. First, the walls of the storage sites for semen and sperm contract. This is known as 'ejaculatory inevitability' – or the point of no return. Most men are aware of these sensations and that there is no going back once they occur. The second phase involves the rhythmic contractions of the muscles around the penile base. These phases result in the pleasurable sensations experienced as orgasm.

Learning to control and delay the ejaculatory response is something that concerns most men. Control of the pubo-coccygeous (PC) muscles is important to this. Learning to

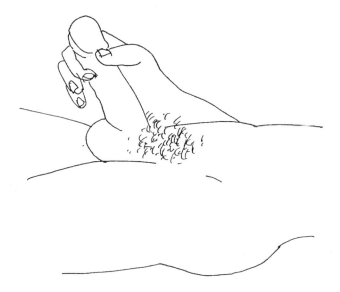

master these muscles can also help men to develop the ability to have multiple orgasms. Yes, it's true! The secret is to practise Kegel exercises (see page 22) on a regular basis. However, if you are worried about problems such as delayed ejaculation, premature ejaculation, lack of ejaculation, or other sexual concerns you should consult your doctor. Not all doctors have training in sexual problems but they can certainly refer you to an expert for any help required.

A simple test in dealing with ejaculatory problems in men is whether you can experience a pleasurable orgasm during masturbation. The same goes for women. If you experience arousal and orgasm during masturbation but have difficulties with a lover, this suggests the difficulties may well have an emotional basis. And that covers a lot of territory! Problems in the relationship, such as fear, anger, or guilt may be affecting your sexual responses.

A sinful taste of Tantric sex

Sinful Sex is not a book of Tantric sex. Many find Tantric principles difficult to embrace. And it's certainly true that if you're going to embrace Tantric sex fully then you really will have to make whole lifestyle/relationship changes, which many are not prepared to do. However, tying in with what I've already said about orgasm and not making it your sole 'goal' in sexual activity, Tantric sex emphasises enjoying the moment not just with your sexual feelings but your emotions, too. Everyone could benefit from embracing this idea so that they slow down and enjoy feeling the path their lovemaking is taking. I'd also like you to know about the basic principles of what Tantric practitioners call the 'whole body orgasm'. Prepare yourself by opening your mind to approaching sexual release with a new attitude.

As your excitement rises and you feel yourself getting near to orgasm, allow your breathing to relax. This is contrary to how most people respond to climax – with quick, shallow breathing. At the same time allow your mind to clear. This means letting any fantasy thoughts – or thoughts of your lover – drift away, creating a blank slate. Now allow your muscles to relax – again, the opposite of how most people behave as they approach orgasm. And finally gaze into your lover's eyes, allowing you both to get lost in the moment. These principles combine to allow your sexual energy to flow out through all your muscles – indeed, your whole body – rather than being focussed in a genital orgasm. Try this a few times when you're in the mood to let go of sexual tension and explore the heightened sense of orgasm it may give you. But don't worry if it doesn't do anything for you!

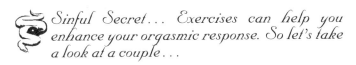 *Sinful Secret... Exercises can help you enhance your orgasmic response. So let's take a look at a couple...*

Sex-ercises for increasing your sexual pleasure
Before you try these sex-ercises, please note: if you have a back or joint disorder or other health problem, you should consult your doctor before embarking on *any* exercises.

Kegel exercises

These exercises were devised by Dr Arnold Kegel to help women regain full pelvic muscle function after childbirth. However, they can also improve sexual enjoyment for both women and men. Women find Kegel exercises not only enhance their ability to reach orgasm but can also be used to stimulate their lover's penis during penetration – something both enjoy! Men find these exercises help to control their plateau period – so increasing their staying power. Both men and women will discover that exercising regularly in this way helps them become multi-orgasmic.

> *Sinful Fact… At the Center for Marital and Sexual Studies in southern California (where else?!) the highest number of orgasms measured in male and female volunteers in one hour was 16 and 134 respectively! But before you go getting any ideas of multiple orgasm heaven — it's quality not quantity that counts!*

This exercise works the PC muscles that run between the pubic bone and the tailbone in women and men. Think of the muscles you'd use if you tried to stop yourself urinating – those are the muscles I'm talking about. Once identified – and you can find them simply by sitting on the toilet and stopping yourself peeing – it's best to build up the number of 'squeezes' you do gradually. Starting with ten repetitions, twice a day, hold this muscle for two to three seconds at a time. Don't go for a tight squeeze – keep it relaxed as you begin. You don't want to try too many with your eagerness! Aim to build to something like three sets of twenty repetitions per day and you'll notice the difference within a couple weeks.

The great thing about working your PC muscles is that you can do it any time it crosses your mind – sitting at your desk, in the bath, in bed, even watching TV. No one can tell you are flexing these important 'friends', so go for it and build your orgasmic ability! Men, in particular, once you've built up the strength of your PC muscles, may want to attempt what one man told me he tried. He used the ingenious method of trying to raise a hand towel up with his semi-erect penis to further build the strength in this muscle. Just don't overdo it!

Now we're into the region of male multiple orgasms. Once you have control of your PC muscles it's in the realms of possibility to learn to reach orgasm without ejaculation. As long as you prevent ejaculation, it's possible to be multi-orgasmic. The fact that male orgasm can be separated from ejaculation was a piece of knowledge recorded first in ancient China and now rediscovered by the West.

This sort of control is best learned through masturbation, where you don't have to worry about your lover's needs. With PC control, it's possible during masturbation to achieve the sensation of orgasm yet stop short of ejaculation. Even if you don't master it, you can have fun practising and you're bound to learn more about your orgasmic response – something that can benefit your lover too. But – and this is a big BUT – if you are anxious about your body or about pleasing your lover, please don't put yourself under additional pressure by trying to learn how to be multi-orgasmic! And that's a message that can't be repeated too often for women too!

Pelvic tilt exercise
To sustain thrusting motions, men and women need a strong lower back and buttocks. The pelvic tilt exercise can help. Lie flat on your back and place your feet flat with your knees bent at a comfortable angle. While holding in your stomach, and without raising your back off the floor, tilt your lower pelvis up towards the ceiling and hold for a count of five. Release, returning your pelvis to a completely flat position. Now repeat for a total of ten repetitions. You may aim to increase these to twenty or so repetitions each day.

The CAT posture
For flexibility in the lower back, try this exercise. Get onto your hands and knees – keeping your knees in line with your

hips. Now, slowly arch your back – the 'cat' – and then roll it down slowly to a flat 'table' posture. Repeat this five times and build up to ten repetitions. The cat is good for loosening your back and aiding flexibility.

Hip rotations

This is another exercise that can enhance your flexibility. Stand with your feet shoulder-width apart and slowly circle your hips. After a few sensual circles, rotate in the opposite direction. This not only improves the suppleness of your joints but also helps you to feel generally relaxed. Try doing a few slow rotations in front of a mirror and imagine yourself circling your hips provocatively in front of your lover.

The Squeeze

To gain even more vaginal control and strength a woman can practise the 'squeeze' by holding a dildo or vibrator (switched off) inside her vagina and squeezing it as if she's practising her Kegel exercises. She'll then be able to grip her partner's penis during penetration to great effect!

General fitness

Generally speaking, the fitter and healthier you are the more likely you are to enjoy your sexual experiences. So, with your doctor's approval, find a form of general physical activity that you enjoy – such as walking, jogging, swimming or a sport of some kind – and practise it regularly. This will improve your health and build your capacity for sexual enjoyment.

Now you have a good understanding of the different stages of sexual pleasure. If you've followed the advice in the first chapter and spoiled yourself with some sinful self-pleasure, maybe next time you will enjoy each stage more as you move through them. Enjoying and treasuring every bit of your sexual response will help you to communicate your needs to your lover – so on we move to 'sinful sex talk'!

Sinful Suggestion . . . The next time something sends a little ripple of excitement through you, or sparks some sexy thoughts, try to identify the different sensations, thoughts and feelings that follow. Getting in tune with these sensations will enhance your sexual responsiveness.

3

Sinful Sex Talk

Now that you understand your own sexual responses, how do you communicate your unique needs to your lover? And how do you begin to find out about theirs? In the introduction I mentioned the 'three Cs' for finding sexual fulfilment – *sexual confidence, communication* and *creativity*. We look at the second of these in this chapter. From the moment you first set eyes on each other and show even a glimmer of interest, you begin to communicate messages about yourselves, without even realising it.

The communication of attraction and sexual interest are revealed by many small signals. The pupils of your eyes dilate, your posture straightens, you subconsciously touch your neckline (if a woman) drawing his eyes to your décolletage. You thrust your thumbs into your belt loops (if a man) to draw her eyes to your 'package'. You play little cat and mouse games with the rest of your body language – crossing and uncrossing your legs, smoothing your hair, tracing a line around the base of your lips, and much, much more.

If you pick up on each other's flirtatious body language and conversation, communication develops in leaps and bounds. You mimic one another's body movements (body mirroring), you move closer, turning towards each other, thereby excluding others from your flirtatious conversation, and you quite literally only have eyes for each other. Sadly though, what starts out with such electricity, all too frequently loses power and fizzles out. It's communication, communication and *more* communication that'll keep the spark of passion alive. And the lack of it that leads to less than satisfying sex.

So, how often do I need to repeat that all-important 'C word'? You and your lover are NOT mind readers, even if at the beginning of your relationship you are so wrapped up in each other that you feel as if you've known each other for ages. You'll have to find ways of communicating your desires and needs if you are to relish a sinful sex life. The earlier in a new relationship that you begin to say and show what you feel and want, the easier it is to continue to do so. This doesn't mean that if you've been together for five, ten or twenty years and feel you don't communicate well sexually that it's too late to start. You can, of course! But it may take more courage and perseverance to change the way you've related to each other sexually over the years.

Before we get started, try this quick quiz to indicate to yourself how much you may – or may not – be communicating sexually already.

The sex-talk quick quiz
1 Have you ever faked orgasm with your present lover (or previous lover, if currently single)?
A Yes, frequently.
B Yes, occasionally.
C No, I wouldn't.

2 In telling your lover they're doing something wrong are you most likely to...
A tell them straight out,
B beat about the bush a bit,
C tell them what they *do right* and ask for more of it.

3 You're dying to try a new sexual technique or position, so would you...

A say that you've always wanted to try 'x, y, and z' and describe it,

B show your lover a photo of what you'd like to try and see if he/she gets the hint,

C offer plenty of praise for what you both do already and sensually coax your lover into the new technique by showing how easy it'd be to 'move into it' or 'add it on' to your lovemaking.

The sex-talk quick quiz key

 Two or three As: You are inhibited in your sexual communication, *at least* with the lover your answers refer to. Your inhibitions are likely to affect your lover's ability to communicate, thereby setting up a negative cycle, unless he/she has got sexual confidence of steel. 'Telling it like it is' – as shown in answers 2A and 3A – sounds tactless to a lover. You may simply think that honesty is the best policy. But straight talking without a huge dose of tact is rarely the best approach when it comes to discussing sexual matters. See 'final words' for more on that subject but take on board the rest of this chapter.

 Two or three Bs: You may be on track for some satisfying sexual communication. You have some of the right ideas – especially if you chose 2B – and you know you shouldn't come straight out with criticism. Yet you haven't got to grips with emphasising all the positives you may have together. Answer 3B may be a good way to stimulate a sexy chat about new things to try. Enhance your starting point by following the advice in the rest of this chapter.

 Two or three Cs: You're well on course for really good sexual communication – at least with your present

lover. You realise that taking your sexual relationship to sinful levels is not about demanding it – it's about coaxing it out of the two of you and enhancing the good you've already got. You should still pay attention to the rest of this chapter, though, as everyone can improve when it comes to sex – but you probably already realise that.

Getting started

The chemistry between two people is unique. And so too is the way they communicate with each other. To make things easier, I'm going to outline sexual communication in its three most manageable forms. Of course, in practice, these often occur in tandem. To help you two connect at a more sexually meaningful level, the following is the most helpful way to structure it.

1 – Actions speak louder than words

Never forget how over 90 per cent of communication is non-verbal. You can harness this and let your body do the 'dirty talk' for you! From the very beginning of foreplay, right through to full sex and climax, you can send out a variety of messages to communicate what you'd like to do or that you'd like to know more about what your partner wants – without saying a word!

The look of lust

To kick things off – say it with a look! Think about how much your face communicates. At a basic level you can tell obvious facial expressions such as anger, sadness and delight. At a deeper level you may pick up on much more subtle messages. Think about the look of longing, of thoughtfulness and of desire. I'm sure you can conjure up facial expressions to accompany these. So use them! Use your expressions to convey to your lover how you're feeling. Especially when in public – one look at each other is worth a thousand words.

The message conveyed in a touch

Let's say you two are on a date and you're feeling attracted
to each other. Use a simple touch to let your companion
know this. Graze your hand across his. Reach out and touch
his (or her) forearm. If seated next to your date, let your
ankle brush his – why do you think we call it 'playing
footsie'? If walking alongside, clasp his arm tightly or
snuggle up underneath it. All these simple touches convey a
greater message – that you *are* interested. And your new
date will want to know that.

Once you've decided to go to bed with your lover –
whether a new or established partner – use non-verbal
communication to guide her (or him) around your body.
And let your lover know she should do the same! Simply
take your partner's hand and move it to where you want to
be touched – this is a huge signal to her. You can then keep
your hand on hers and move it to stimulate the erogenous
zone she's touching in the way you want it to be touched.
You could even take her finger and manipulate it – showing
how you want your partner to move it over your body. Now
slip your hand under hers and show her you want her to
guide your hand to her pleasure zones.

Body hugging is another approach. Entwine your limbs so
that your body touches his in a pleasurable way and
'wriggle' about a bit so he knows you're enjoying the sensation as well. As you clasp him tightly, shift your body as
his hands roam over you to help nudge his hands to where
you want them to be.

Using moist lips, kiss the inside of his palm and then place
his damp palm where you'd like it. Or suck his fingers
suggestively – hinting at your desire for oral pleasure. And
place your fingers in his mouth. Simply enjoy knowing that
by moving your hands and body – and encouraging him to
do the same – you can communicate at an intimate level.

2 – Preverbal sex talk

You don't have to use words to communicate – you may use

the sounds of lust and love. There is a repertoire of sexy
sounds you can make to encourage your lover to keep doing
what he's doing right or to show him he has reached an
erogenous zone as his hands glide over your body.

Letting out little sighs, moans and groans will give out
signals that you're enjoying what your lover is doing. And
if you stop making such noises, perhaps because your
partner has changed what he's doing, he will hopefully get
the message and resume doing what you found so
pleasurable. After all – hearing your sinfully sexy noises is
a big turn-on for him, too! You should fine-tune your
listening skills, too, so that you get to know his noises. You
may both soon get to know the telltale sounds that indicate
the other one is reaching the point of no return – for
example, his utterances or breathing may change at this
point. This is particularly helpful if a man needs slowing
down, perhaps because you are not quite ready to orgasm
and would like him to last a little longer. So listen carefully
as you get to know your lover – enjoy the sounds he makes
when you're turning him on – and give him loads of
encouragement through your own!

3 – Talking dirty

I'm going to start with what seems the most obvious area of
sexual communication – talking to each other. Yet this is
probably the toughest thing for some people to do. But
what's ever stopped me from throwing you in at the deep
end in order to enhance your sex life?

The art of talking about sex not only involves the words
you use but also *how* you say them. In terms of how you say
something to a lover, there are a few key principles to keep
in mind at all times. People are extremely sensitive to spoken
words that pertain to the physical and emotional act of
lovemaking. Just put yourself on the receiving end of a
critical-sounding voice, or even a nervous or anxious tone of
voice. People make a mental leap and assume that if you're
nervous about talking to them about a sexual issue then

there's probably *even more* to it that you're not telling them. That's how paranoid we are about our sexual performance!

What's the best tone of voice to use when talking sex? This depends on whether you're trying to change something that's not working or trying to add something new to your lovemaking.

Talking about something that's NOT working

 When trying to change something that's not working sexually you should always use your most confident tone of voice. Confidence conveys optimism and with the profound sensitivity people feel about changing aspects of their behaviour you need to be optimistic that he or she can improve.

 As well as confidence, use a sensual tone. Practise lowering your voice slightly as well as softening its tone, and slowing its pace – you'll already be sounding more sensual. Anything sounds better when it's said like that!

 Always choose a *positive* to start with. For example, if you find the way your lover kisses you is a big turn-on but his (or her) touch is a major turn-off – begin with the turn-on. Try something like, 'I *love* the way you kiss me – it feels so sensual. I'd be in heaven if you tried touching me with your fingers the way your lips brush my skin.' Try to move seamlessly from the positive to the negative you are trying to change. Think it through before you speak – but that should be true at all times!

 Suggest a positively sexy substitute. Sometimes people try something sexually that doesn't particularly work for one or the other but doesn't appear to 'fail' completely either. So, one lover may initiate it again. As sexual activity is fluid and changes over time it's perfectly possible to suggest the next step on from whatever you tried and didn't like. For example, if your lover turned you over from Spoons (see page 63) into the Resting Dog (see page 76) and you found this position just didn't *do it* for you, instead of communicating as much, you could simply say, 'Let's move into good old-fashioned doggy style.' Once you've made the change to something you find more satisfying, make a point of saying, 'Isn't this great?' Your lover will associate this new technique or position with your enthusiasm.

Encouraging something new

 Even when you are simply trying to encourage a little sexual experimentation, you need to be aware of how you make the suggestion so that you do not seem to be implying that you are bored or unhappy with what you two have been doing. Be playful and use that soft and sensual tone of voice (and this goes for both men and women!). Tell your lover you've fantasised about X, Y or Z – and you'd love to try it with him.

 Get out a sex advice book (*Sinful Sex*) and share it with her. Show her the page that has something on it you want to try – such as a sex position or oral sex suggestion. Bring the book to bed when you're both feeling sexy and say, 'Take a look at this. Would you enjoy that?' This gives your lover a sense that you really do care about her enjoying new techniques.

 Be a bit of a tease and turn it into a game. Say things like, 'Can you guess what I'd like to try? It involves me getting in some sexy knickers, putting on a little mood music and you being my audience…'

Communicating over serious sexual issues

 There are times when all the hints in the world, all the subtle sensuous dirty talk, or confident vocal tones won't help when something needs changing at a deeper level. Try some of the following techniques to ensure that communication over such sensitive issues goes as smoothly as possible.

 Ask your lover what he/she thinks about the issue/ technique/routine/position you hope to change. By asking for his opinion first you are starting the dialogue *respectfully*. Then really listen to what he says and try to empathise with his point of view. When it is your turn to express an opinion you're bound to be more tactful.

 If it's really serious, *don't* discuss it in the bedroom. Otherwise the bedroom itself may become 'associated' with any negativity in the conversation.

 Never employ the 'you always–I always' argument. For example, you may feel that you initiate sex 98 per cent of the time. This leaves you feeling that your lover simply isn't bothered – and that doesn't make you feel desirable. But once you start bandying about such phrases people tend to get on the defensive. 'Oh, so I always do that, do I?!' and so it spins into a negative cycle. Banish words like 'always' and 'never' from your conversations about sex and you'll get much further.

 Suggest trade-offs when trying to get over a sexual issue. Using the above example, if one of you tends to be the initiator of sexual encounters then talk about how you might turn it into a bit of a game. For example, suggest that the person who is less likely to suggest sex tries a role-play that turns him or her on. He may pretend to be your new boss summoning you for a late-night 'work' session, for example. By appealing to his fantasy life you may spark his confidence to take the lead. Whatever, be open to your partner's suggestions. Don't rule them out without thinking. Often when an issue builds up over sex, underlying anger develops that makes it almost impossible to accept what the other might suggest. But it will benefit *you* if you do listen without jumping in!

 Never see a problem as 'You v. Me' but always 'We'! When you allocate blame, and see only your own side of a problem, the issue becomes 'You v. Me'. But if you see yourselves as a couple – 'We' – against a 'shared problem', you'll have a far more positive outcome!

 Many couples find condoms one of the most difficult subjects to communicate about. Talking about condoms should come early in your relationship because you'll find out a lot about your potential lover this way. Using condoms can be fun – you can experiment together and even play games such as 'hunt the condom' when he's wearing a luminous one. There are so many kinds (and sizes!) to choose from to ensure that the fit and feel are right for you. A great tip is to drip a little water-based lubricant into the condom to give the man a gorgeous wet sensation. Remember always to follow the instructions on the pack.

The sinfulness of sexy nicknames!
It's time for you and your lover to have lots of fun and give each other some sexy nicknames – particularly esteem-boosting ones. Call him 'Mr Big' or 'Mr Lover-man'. Call her 'Sex Goddess' or 'Gorgeous Lips'! This will help you gain confidence to use naughty words, which some find hard to do. You can then carry this into your lovemaking. Really go to town, particularly in fantasy play, by getting as dirty as you wish – as long as your lover finds it a turn-on too!

Don't forget you can practise, when on your own, naming parts of your lover's and your own anatomy! Some people are frightened of saying words such as 'penis' or 'vagina', and need to familiarise themselves with the way it sounds rolling off their lips. With practice you'll find you can speak frankly – and sexily – with your lover!

 Sinful Secret... Remember – as one lover brings out the best in you, allowing you to freely express your sexuality, another may make you feel inhibited. Similarly, the way you behave and communicate your feelings will have different effects on different lovers, too!

Final words
There are some times when straight-talking honesty is the best policy in sexual communication. For example:
 If your lover is causing you physical pain – tell it straight.

If your lover hasn't picked up on any of your helpful hints.

 If issues such as your lover's personal hygiene are turning you off.

 If you can't talk about safer sex with your lover – maybe you shouldn't be sleeping with them!

Meaningful sexual communication is a wonderful thing that can deepen your experiences, enhance your intimacy and improve your relationship. Treat your lover and love-making like a precious gift and you can't go wrong when you decide to talk about it.

4

Sinfully Unforgettable Foreplay

Foreplay begins long before you hit the sack (or sofa – or *wherever* you end up making love). In fact, I call this aspect of your sexual relationship *before-play* because the emotional mood between the two of you will dictate how susceptible you are to initiating foreplay. If there've been arguments over bills, children, etc., then quite frankly neither of you will be interested. That aside, the best foreplay begins with a knowing look, a flirty conversation, and some 'scene-setting' – not necessarily in that order. Foreplay builds anticipation in your most important sex organ – your mind. If only we could be like the Hindu god *Shiva*, whose fore- and sex-play with his 'consort' *Parvati* were so energetic as to frighten other gods!

Of course, some foreplay can be as fast and furious as some sex is quick and passionate. You two may not have been thinking about sex then something suddenly arouses you – such as a scene in a film, a passage in a book – and away you go, giving suggestive looks and making suggestive noises, before tumbling straight into lovemaking.

Foreplay can also be something that builds but doesn't

reach a sexual climax. You and your lover may touch and caress each other sensuously, knowing all along that one of you has got to leave for, say, an appointment. This can leave you with a delicious feeling of anticipation, waiting for the moment when you can pick up where you left off and resume the foreplay.

Engaging in foreplay means you get a 'feel' for the sort of lovemaking mood that your partner is in. This makes use of the methods of communication discussed in the previous chapter in all its more subtle forms to gauge what your partner desires, as well as showing your lover what you're in the mood for.

For example, your lover may grip your hand urgently and place it over his penis or her clitoral region, suggesting he or she would like you to use a faster pace than usual. Or your partner may slow you down by stopping you from moving your hands to her genital hot spots too quickly. Wriggling with quiet pleasure in response to a gentle fondling of the breasts or a nuzzling of the neck suggests a desire for a languid pace.

If you're with someone new then the foreplay he or she gives and desires will say a lot about that person as a lover. For example, if you find he yields to your foreplay and allows you to guide, this suggests he may find taking the lead – or sharing it – difficult. You may need to build his confidence by asking him what feels good as you touch him. Of course, your lover may be the king (or queen) of foreplay and start kissing you from your neck down to your toes – pure heaven – so enjoy it!

Foreplay is very important for a woman in helping her sexual arousal build to the point where she can reach orgasm. As noted in Chapter Two, most women need about 20–30 minutes of stimulation to reach climax. Foreplay is an erotic *entrée* to this! Some men also need more time and don't want to rush into penetration, fully enjoying the excitement foreplay gives them, too.

A sinfully delicious way to start foreplay is by flirting. A lot of flirting is about teasing the other into a state of sexual arousal. Flirting can be very subtle, leaving you unsure where it's going – and that's the teasing part of it. You may be sitting enjoying a TV programme or a movie at the cinema, and slowly you begin to caress your lover's inner arm with your nails, all the while pretending to be engrossed in the programme. He wonders, 'Does she know how she's teasing me?' Or you greet your lover with a 'hello' kiss and allow your hand to gently linger on her lower back, making a soft and sensual circular movement. She is left feeling, 'What does this touch mean?' Flirting can be fairly outrageous and quite straightforward. For example, if your lover is bending over you could come up behind him and skilfully caress his genitals through his clothing while telling him that imagining his naked buttocks gives you a tingle between your legs.

You can continue to build this sense of sexual tension for as long as you wish and in the way you wish – with sexy chat and touches and kisses of various sorts. The important issue to remember is that foreplay should be fun, it should communicate your longings and indicate how these will be fulfilled, and make you both feel good – and sinfully sexy!

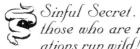 *Sinful Secret... The most sinful lovers are those who are not afraid to let their imaginations run wild!*

Let's begin at the beginning

Along with flirting, the best starting point for your foreplay is good old-fashioned romance. Now I know I've just mentioned that foreplay can be fast and furious, so you may wonder why I mention romance. The point is, if you and your lover are in some sort of relationship – or at least, not strangers – you should both be generating romance to keep your relationship loving and lively. And romantic gestures will make you both feel good and get you in the mood for fantastic foreplay. I've created a list of simple romantic gestures. You can pick and choose the ones that appeal to you – and, hopefully, they'll set your imagination alight.

Simple romantic gestures –

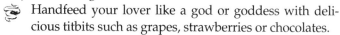

- Handfeed your lover like a god or goddess with delicious titbits such as grapes, strawberries or chocolates.
- Turn a cuddle into a sensual neck and back massage and give your partner a blissful experience.
- Create a love-tape of your lover's favourite love songs and present it to him.
- Write a loving, affectionate and sexy note for your lover and leave it somewhere you know she'll find it during the day.
- Send a love letter. You don't have to fill pages – just one or two lines saying how you feel about her speaks volumes and will make her feel so good.
- Send a text or e-mail that simply says that you're thinking of him at that moment.
- The next time you have dinner together, light a few candles, put on some soft music and show your lover you want to make her feel good.
- Offer to go out on an errand for your lover and come back with a surprise gift – it only needs to be a small present yet the gesture seems big on caring!
- Find the inner child in yourself and your lover – head for the park and play on the swings, taking it in turn to push each other. Buy two water pistols for a play fight – it'll turn into a wet T-shirt contest.
- As your lover walks in through the door, guide her to the bathroom for a warm relaxing bath – having made sure it's candle-lit and full of fragrant bubbles.
- Make breakfast, lunch or dinner for your lover – when they're in bed.
- Compliment him – telling him what it is you love – *or lust after –* him for.
- Ask your lover to help you set the table, and then give him a big smoochy kiss on it.
- Make a surprise visit to your lover at work and whisk her off for a little lunch-time flirting.
- Give him a calendar for the rest of the year. On the first day of each month, write something naughty to bring a wicked smile to his face.

I think you get the point. Romantic gestures will get your lover in the mood to respond to foreplay. In modern society, we forget that it is the small things that make us feel good. We want to know our partner has given a little extra thought to bringing us happiness. The great lovers of history recognised the fantastic effect that a romantic gesture could have. Casanova used to send chocolate love tokens to the woman he was pursuing. The tokens were individually shaped to represent something important to her.

All of the above add to your romantic environment. Don't forget the importance of scene-setting if you're getting in the mood at home. The television should be switched off – unless you're watching something erotic! Turn the lights down low, perhaps adding a few scented candles – ylang-ylang and musk are renowned for their aphrodisiac properties – and put on some romantic music, if you wish.

Gestures such as offering to wash your lover's hair – sensually and lovingly – also set the scene for wonderful foreplay. Couples don't often engage in this but it can be heaven for both of you and lead on to other things such as water play and gentle touching. Once the hair is washed and you're towelling the excess water off, you can move on to enjoy more erotic pleasures. For example, hair washing can lead to – *or* begin with – a shared bath. Try soaking in a warm bath together, again with a few candles for subtle lighting, gently washing each other's bodies, trailing your fingers down to each other's genitals – this can give you both enormous pleasure.

Sealed with a kiss
Once you've got into the great habit of stimulating romance, foreplay flows much more easily. Kissing forms a wonderful part of foreplay. The fact that the lips and mouth form the vessels for our 'source of life' plays a part in this. We derive physical sustenance through them and sexual sustenance too! Desmond Morris postulated that in early human cultures food would be chewed by mothers and then 'kissed'

into the mouths of their children – providing nourishment and creating an intimate mother–child bond.

In our modern culture, mothers don't provide food by this method but they still kiss and touch the heads of their infants with their lips. The infants use their lips to suckle at the breast or bottle – deriving much contentment and pleasure through their mouths. As we grow into young lovers, we recreate such early and comforting intimacy by exploring one another's mouths with our tongues. And penetration of the mouth with the tongue also symbolises the penetration of full lovemaking to come!

What's important to remember about kissing is that the various techniques I am about to describe can be used to *sinful effect* all around your lover's body. In Chapter Six, I focus on genital kissing with lots more suggestions. Kissing with loving care, tenderness and passion can actually send tingles of pleasure down the abdomen to the genitals – so no one should ever be under the illusion that kissing doesn't count!

 Sinful Sense... Unless you've both been sharing a meal laced with garlic, or other strong flavours, always ensure your breath is fresh before you touch your lover's lips with yours.

Sinful, blissful kisses
There are so many variations of kissing that I'll describe a few favourites that anyone can use confidently.

The Beginner's Kiss
A simple meeting of the lips. Your lips may brush against each other or gently press together. Done with finesse this can be a fantastic starting point. A variation of this is to 'swirl' your lips slowly around your lover's. Relax, let go and allow your lips to roam over and around your lover's mouth – real bliss with little effort!

The Sliding Kiss
The tongue moves gently back and forth or in and out. A perfect kiss, too, for gently 'sliding' erotic food – such as sauces and creams – off your lover's body as your foreplay develops.

The good old French Kiss
With open mouths, your tongues gently probe and swirl against the delicate skin inside the mouth.

The Vacuum Kiss
Allow your lips to relax and encircle your partner's lips with your own. Apply a gentle sucking motion that pulls on the much-neglected outer rim of the lips. Release the vacuum seal and then reapply. You're taking control and your lover's lips will yield to yours. You may also apply the 'vacuum' to a single lip – upper or lower. Also use the 'vacuum' on your lover's tongue during 'French' kissing, which will feel like heaven. If you apply the 'vacuum' more firmly to your partner's body it'll become a lovebite – see below.

The Medieval Necklet
Said to be enjoyed by knights of the realm when medieval ladies wore low-cut necklines. Gently circle your lover's neck with a series of kisses, moving from the lower neck just behind the ear, around the breastbone and finishing back behind the other ear. Both men and women enjoy the slow circular pattern being traced along this delicate skin.

The Naughty Dog
A passionate, earthy kiss, particularly good for larger erogenous zones such as the neck, breasts, abdomen and inner thigh. Let your mouth open loosely and allow your tongue to relax and 'lap' at your lover's body. This feels incredible when applied from the lower part of the breast up to the tip of the nipple – the tongue just flicking the nipple as the 'lapping' motion finishes.

The Lush Lap
More controlled than the Sloppy Dog, this kiss still involves
a lapping motion with your tongue, but is more contained
and controlled, with your lips kept close to your lover's skin.
With your lips parted, use a firm, slow lap of the tongue
pressed to her (or his) flesh, lips or mouth. Again, this kiss
puts you in control and feels incredibly sexy to a lover who
likes to yield to your moves.

The Eastern Swirl and Poke
This may be applied to the lips or the body. Relax your lips
and allow your tongue to swirl and poke. Alternating these
swirling and poking sensations feels wonderful.

The Mediterranean Flick
Said to originate from Latin lovers who flicked little beads of
sweat from their lover's body during long hot summers of
passion. Using a gentle flick of the tongue, you cover your
lover's lips, cheeks, neck – in fact, anywhere you please –
using delicate little flicks. This is perfect for the nipples and
around the tummy button.

The Snake
Moving on from the 'flick', allow your tongue to flick, lap,
poke and generally imitate that of a snake. This can take place
while French kissing but can also be used all over your lover's
body. It feels fantastic moving up and down the shaft of the
penis or outer labia (but we'll come to all that in Chapter Six!).

The Droplet
Try experimenting with this in the heat of passion. If you're
on top of your lover and kissing passionately, withdraw
your lips slightly from his and allow a few droplets of your
saliva to drip gently into his mouth.

The Stretch
When French kissing, stretch your tongue up to rub the roof
of your lover's mouth. People rarely focus on this area, yet

the sensations your tongue can create here can be quite explosive.

The Butterfly Kiss
Using your eyelashes, gently flutter them across your lover's lips, eyelids, cheeks, neck and, when kissing the breasts, on the nipples too.

The Lover's Pass
When you want to pass something in a sensual way to your lover – perhaps a piece of chocolate, fruit or ice – simply hold it gently between your lips and allow your mouth to touch his. Then, using your tongue, push the item into his mouth.

Foreplay can build to an extraordinary level of passion through kissing. You and your lover may feel you're drawing the very heart and soul out of each other. Your kissing seems to quench a thirst that doesn't require water. Enjoy the moment.

Increase the heat with some gentle love 'bites'. This sounds such an adolescent thing to do but you needn't worry about leaving bruises on your lover's neck, breasts, thighs or wherever! Instead you can build up the tension with a stronger 'vacuum' – releasing his or her skin before any real mark is made. If he loves the sensation but doesn't want to go to work with a love bite – simply dive below the neckline and 'bite' him where he wants.

 Sinful Secret… Lovebiting done well, with an attitude of being-in-charge, begins to border on the dominant-submissive theme — very exciting. Read more about it in Chapter Seven.

Your foreplay (and more) treasure chest
Every bedroom should contain a 'treasure chest' (lockable if you've got children around) containing your own sinful set

of pleasure and foreplay 'enhancers'. The following should be readily available:

- Lubricants and massage oils. If you're using condoms use only water-based types. Oil-based 'lubes' can damage condoms. Also, be careful to avoid any oil getting inside the vagina. This may cause irritation.
- Sex toys you enjoy – I'll go into these in more detail in Chapter Nine – but your treasure chest is a great place to keep them.
- A blindfold – preferably of soft, satiny material for comfort. These enhance pleasure as described in Chapter Seven.
- Erotica to read to each other or films you find stimulating.
- Stockings or soft ties for a bit of bondage play – again described in Chapter Seven – and a pair of handcuffs.
- A feather or 'brush' for playful touching. More on this in Chapter Seven, too.
- Little sexy surprises for your lover. A silky thong, some surprise stockings, fun chocolates or 'love dice' (see page 159).
- Dental dams, cling film, and condoms for safer sex. Don't forget some latex gloves for sensual stimulation of the anal area without scratching your lover with your nails.
- A box of luxury tissues and/or a soft cloth for 'cleaning up'.
- And in the fridge, erotic edibles that you love, such as cream, yoghurt, jam, sauces, honey and jelly. You'll find that sticky things such as jelly and honey feel fabulous on the genitals when gently warmed. Test the temperature on your inner wrist and then smooth it on and lap it off.

Touching in foreplay

I cover genital touching and kissing in Chapter Six and other special touching techniques in Chapter Seven. Here, I'll cover the more general form of body touching used in foreplay. Touching in foreplay is mainly about pressure and style. I think it's always best to start gently and build up to the level of sensation your lover enjoys, rather than start too roughly and have him or her draw back in surprise. Of course, you may experience a passionate moment – maybe one of you has been away – and you seize each other and tumble to the bed or floor and grasp and 'claw' at each other's clothes. Real movie stuff! In such moments, your foreplay may be brisk and firm from the start.

As you touch your lover, listen to his or her 'love sounds' and *ask* how it feels. Don't forget the erogenous-zone maps covered in Chapter One. All of these zones may be activated during foreplay! You should focus on your lover's favourites but bear in mind that exploring other areas will keep your lovemaking alive. What's important is to get away from the feeling that you're 'joining the dots' – that is, you're sticking religiously to the advice of a sex guide (even *Sinful Sex*!), following it to the letter rather than going with the flow of your desires and those of your partner.

Begin with your fingertips, swirling over the nape of your lover's neck. Lift his hair gently to kiss underneath it. Always touch the scalp and hair gently, asking your lover if he'd like you to increase the pressure. Breathe gently against the back of his ears and skim your lips over the tender skin of his earlobe. Kiss and suck the lobe gently and never speak directly into his ear – ouch! Instead whisper very quietly what you'd like to do to him and how much you're enjoying the moment. Yield to his touch, too. Both of you should enjoy the initiation of foreplay!

While kissing the neck region, beneath her hair, you may also offer to comb her hair. This can feel very intimate. To get truly sinful, though, offer to comb or brush her genital hair 'later on'. Even if your partner is neatly trimmed you can get seriously sexy by gently combing this area.

Use a number of fingertip techniques to arouse your lover. Try circular, gentle massage moves, fluttering, light drumming, stroking and rubbing techniques. Let your imagination run wild and allow your hands to roam in a way that feels natural and that your lover is enjoying.

 Sinful Secret... A woman's skin is very sensitive. Not only is it much more delicate than a man's, it has twice as many nerve endings. If your hands are covered in calluses or your nails are ragged, running your hands up and down your partner's soft skin will not feel nice at all. If your hands need attention, prepare them before making love!

As you move on to other erogenous zones – the breasts, abdomen, thighs and knees – don't forget those sadly neglected zones that rarely get pleasured, such as the inside of the elbow or wrist, behind the knees, and all over the ankles and toes. Start to introduce some of the kisses described above – but be subtle. Don't dive straight on your lover's nipples with the Snake or Flick. Instead, *tantalise* her – that's what sinful foreplay is all about! Flick from the inner elbow, up along the arm, and then down and around the armpit to the ribs. From here, make your way up the side of the breast following a lazy trail to the nipple.

Signalling things should go a step further
As your arousal grows, you can use signals to show that you want to take foreplay to the next level. Take your lover's hand and suck his fingers slowly and sensuously, one at a time. Gaze into his eyes for an intimate bond and whisper how fantastic you're feeling. Or use some dirty talk to take the mood to an earthy level. Perhaps now is the time to move on to some genital touching – maybe so far you have taken your foreplay to the edge of the genitals but held back from the pleasure of actually touching them.

Touching during foreplay may be done from many positions and often starts when you two are standing and kissing. But it's also easy to fondle and kiss each other if you are lying or sitting side by side – especially when you're cuddling in the Spoons position (see page 63) while watching TV.

Now for some fantastic touching. If a couple happen to start their love-play while sitting on a sofa or chair, the woman can ease herself off of it, turn around and lean on to the chair while her partner kneels behind her – almost as if going into Doggy style for lovemaking. He can then fondle her from behind, perhaps commanding her to spread her legs (even though still clothed) for him to work his fingers up and down her inner thighs. During foreplay, we often say or do things that suggest sexual techniques to come. Here 'commanding' may suggest some light bondage later!

'V' is for victory!
A sinfully erotic genital technique to use on a woman is what I call the 'V' for victory sign. This works best if you kneel or stand behind your partner and reach round her hip or waist to place your hand between her legs. Make your index and middle fingers into a 'V' shape and slide these fingers to either side of the clitoris, running down over the outer labia and pointing towards the perineum. The underside of your fingers will now be stimulating the clitoral 'arms'. Gently move your fingers up and down – drawing the clitoral hood lightly up and down as you do so, thereby providing very gentle clitoral stimulation. You may also circle the fingertips gently while in the 'V' sign – so that the whole area is gently stimulated. Avoid touching the clitoris directly, then you'll keep her gasping for more!

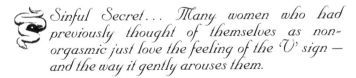

Sinful Secret... Many women who had previously thought of themselves as non-orgasmic just love the feeling of the 'V' sign — and the way it gently arouses them.

From the 'V' sign, take her lead for genital fondling. She may not want any direct stimulation of her clitoris until she's really lubricated. In fact, some women may not be able to take any direct finger or tongue stimulation at all – preferring the palm of the hand or, during oral sex, the lips. Chapter Six contains many suggestions for you. The man, too, may wish to be touched in specific ways. This is the perfect point in foreplay to whisper and ask what your lover would really like.

The Swan
The 'swan' is a great way to stimulate your partner's penis and testicles when you've been roaming around his other erogenous zones. Imagine your thumb and fingers coming together in the shape of the old-fashioned shadow puppet – the 'swan'. This is great for gently clasping the testicles between the 'beak-like' shape formed by your fingers. *Gently* pull them a little. Now open your fingers up again and swirl them around his inner thighs. Then stop and stroke his perineum. Next, apply the 'swan' as an upwards movement from the base of his penis, pulling his foreskin (if he has one) *gently* up over his glans. If he's circumcised it is better to gently flutter your fingertips down the shaft of his penis. Now clasp the base of his shaft and gently and rhythmically 'massage' the base of it, pulling upwards only if he wants that stimulation. Circumcised men vary tremendously in the degree of stimulation they need – some have 'deadened' sensitivity and need a much firmer touch while others are very sensitive. Always ask your lover how he wants you to touch him.

 Sinful Secret... For those men who worry about the size of their penis and are unsure whether or not they'll pleasure their lover – become the king of unforgettable foreplay and you'll be the best lover she's ever had!

Erotic '8'
This massage technique can be used on a man or woman. Get your lover to lie on her back while you warm some massage oil in your hands. Kneel astride her thighs and lean forwards placing both hands just below her neckline and above her breastbone. Start a slow, smooth path with your

oiled hands outwards and down either side of her ribcage, just skimming the edges of her breasts. Now slowly and sensuously draw your hands in to meet at the navel. Pause a moment before recommencing the outwards sweep of the figure '8' down around her outer hips, your hands meeting over her pubis. Gently kneed her pubis and even allow your fingers to wander over her genitals before starting the sweeping motion back up to her navel, and onwards. Repeat the Erotic '8' movement as many times as you wish.

 Sinful Suggestion . . . Now have your lover turn over onto her stomach and do the 'Erotic 8' around her shoulder blades and then down, meeting at her lower back. From here, flare out again around her buttocks. Reaching between her upper thighs, stroke her perineum a few times before starting the movement back up her body.

Thai body massage

This is so named because many Thai masseuses encourage skin-on-skin contact during a massage with their clients to tempt them into asking for 'extras'. The Thai body massage consists of gently rubbing your naked body over your lover's bare skin. It is ideal if you are both kissing, with one lying slightly on top of the other. Rise up on your hands and gently swish your chest and abdomen over your lover's body. This feels particularly erotic on a woman's breasts – skin against skin. If you have the arm strength you may also move your abdomen and hips across your lover's body.

But don't stop there, a woman can now get sinfully sexy by 'massaging' her lover with her genitals! Open your legs and glide your labia across his abdomen gently touching his genitals. Then move across his penis and thighs, allowing your labia to 'touch down' momentarily so he can feel your wetness. The skin-on-skin contact feels amazingly sensual!

Oriental hair massage
Many Oriental cultures perfect sensuality in ways we barely think of. The long fine hair that many women of the East cultivate serves a fantastic purpose in foreplay. Ask him to remove his clothes (if he hasn't done so already!) and, once you've been kissing and caressing for a while, get him to lie face down on the bed or sofa. Kneeling above him, gently glide your lovely tresses down his back and over his buttocks. Continue on down his thighs. Next, turn him over and continue the hair 'massage' across his penis and lower abdomen. A man's less sensitive skin can come alive with an Oriental hair massage.

The Roman Bath
You can try this while sharing a bath, or when sitting on the floor with your back against a sofa, or in bed against the bed-head during foreplay. One of you sits behind the other and reaches around to fondle. For example, the man can sit behind his lover in the bath, with her bottom between his legs close up to his genitals. He massages her breasts and genitals from behind using a cupping, massaging or tweaking motion. One way to do this is to use his whole hand to cup her breasts, then gently massage them. From here he can run his hands down her abdomen and between her thighs. She may gently 'grind' and wiggle her buttocks back into his genital region. If she's sitting behind him, she can reach around to massage his chest and then reach down to cup his genitals. It generates a different feel when touching each other while sitting Roman Bath style – without any eye-to-eye contact. I can only guess that it got this name because so much naughtiness went on in ancient Roman baths. Perhaps sex play was often done from behind so the participants couldn't really see each other.

Introducing something 'extra'
If you two are sipping champagne – or any tipple – your lover can pour a little down your breasts and lick it off gently. Or you could dribble some into his belly button and

lap it up – no worries about 'fluff' if you two have just bathed together!

Turn your lover over and continue to dribble something down her upper back to lick from between her shoulder blades – an incredibly sensitive spot – some lovers can't even tolerate such powerful stimulation. Next, move down with your tongue to the top of her buttocks. This area is very sensitive. Massage the buttocks using circular strokes, slowly moving lower and lower until you can start to stimulate the genital area.

Take control and gently open her thighs to allow you to tickle her with your tongue or a sex toy (more to come on sex toys in Chapter Nine!). Or ask your lover to keep her back to you and rise up on all fours so you can reach around from behind for some more 'Roman Bath style' stimulation. Her breasts, chest and genitals will be more exposed to your foreplay activities. And you can apply skin-to-skin contact by gently rubbing your chest across her back and buttocks.

Don't forget your lover's feet and toes. Caressing these can release an enormous amount of tension. The more relaxed your lover feels, the more he or she is able to enjoy your lovemaking. Start by kissing and licking down his body and legs all the way down to his feet, or ask him to lean back comfortably against pillows. Now take a foot in your hand, and using massage oil, stroke his toes one at a time from the base to the tip. Next, take the ball of the foot and massage it with circular motions. Move upwards to the instep and back to the heel. If your lover has bathed you may want to kiss/suck his toes (called 'shrimping', and no, I'm not going to make jokes about this being a 'royal' technique!) and flick your tongue along his instep – sinfully delicious!

Taking off your clothes
Believe it or not, taking off clothes during foreplay can be extremely challenging for many people – women especially often have inhibitions about how they look. Early on in a relationship, this reticence can be a real stumbling block –

yielding comical moments new lovers would rather not have! You could strip off in stages as you tease your lover, or dive under the sheets for cover before you have even begun foreplay – it all depends on your levels of body confidence. You should use your new-found sinful sex-talking ways to sound out how your lover feels about undressing – unless of course she has no inhibitions and has dropped her clothes from the moment you both were alone!

A good guide is to start undoing items as kissing progresses – taking everything off all at once can disturb the mood too much. Make taking off your lover's clothes part of your delicious foreplay by slowly and sensuously undoing zips, buttons and fastenings. Then plant a sexy kiss on her skin as the clothing falls open. Resume touching and kissing before removing another item. Enjoy this moment, as if you're unwrapping a most erotic gift, and you can't go wrong.

Sexy underwear (on men too!) presents a perfect opportunity to take foreplay to a higher level. For example, if she's wearing a slinky bra he can kiss the soft skin of her forearm up to the strap, and as he pulls the strap down, gently kiss the skin there. She can pull down the cups of her bra to expose her nipples to his lips. It hints at what's to come but doesn't give the whole game away. If she's wearing suspenders he can gently flick them and then kiss the skin that he has flicked as he undoes them. She, of course, can kiss down his abdomen and then up his thighs before sliding a finger under his pants. Pulling up any elastic allows her to slither her tongue seductively up into the area the pants cover. Savour these moments of sinful pleasure when undressing each other.

Mutual masturbation

Mutual masturbation is a fabulous way to learn what the other loves. It's sinfully sexy for a woman to watch her lover pleasure himself – and it gives her the opportunity to show off to her lover! If you've been engaged in foreplay and feel the urge to touch yourself, simply move away slightly and begin. Signal to your lover that you'd like him to watch you or to touch himself at the same time. If he seems shy, let him know how exciting it'd be to watch. But don't press a new lover too much if he feels inhibited.

Final words

I think you'll have gathered by now that the foreplay you engage in can be sinfully varied and sophisticated – or simple – depending on the mood you are both in and the time you have available. This chapter is, of course, only the beginning, giving you a variety of ideas to try as a starting point. It's also not an exhaustive list but a selection of things most people can excel at – and vary with their own unique ideas. Next, you'll find positions to move into once you've been pleasuring each other with loads of wonderful foreplay!

5

Sinful Positions & Places

The third 'C' of sexual fulfilment mentioned in the introduction actually permeates this whole book. I'm talking about sexual *creativity*. You can be creative in the way you pleasure yourself, the way you communicate with your partner, and a whole host of other ways, but in this chapter it refers to *creative sexual positions*. And here you really can start seeing your own creativity in action.

How confident you are about being inventive with different positions depends on several factors. Many women have expressed to me their concerns that a position may draw attention to an aspect of their body that they're not happy with. For example, if a woman doesn't like her bottom she may shy away from Doggy style, where her rear is completely on show to her lover. You can be sure, though, that her lover won't feel the same way about it! So this is where a man can really boost a woman's confidence by telling her how gorgeously sexy she looks from this angle.

On the other hand, men often worry about being over-stimulated (and ejaculating too quickly) or being under-stimulated (and not achieving enough sensation and friction to stimulate them to climax). We often speak of women failing to reach orgasm owing to a lack of the right stimulation during penetration. But it is less well known that a man also needs the type and level of stimulation that is tailored to his particular size and shape. If we look at penetrative sex in purely physical terms, it enables a man to bring himself to orgasm inside a woman's vagina and a women to masturbate against the man's pelvis, pubic bone and penis to achieve full pleasure.

Both sexes worry that their suggestions for alternative sex positions may be rejected by a lover. Women in particular can be concerned that their ideas may lead men to infer that they aren't happy with the sex they are having. But now that you've read Chapter Three you will know that such worries should never hold you back from communicating your wishes to your lover!

It's important to remember that different positions suit different lovers, depending on their size, shape, and other factors such as strength and flexibility – as well as the obvious – preference! If you're a man who is, say, 1.9m (6ft 3in) tall and your lover is 1.6m (5ft 2in) tall you may find, for example, that the classic Missionary position is tricky because your face ends up being so far above hers that you can't gaze into each other's eyes. However, if you are a creative couple and reverse the missionary so she's on top and wriggles slightly upwards on your pelvis into the 'CAT' position (Coital Alignment Technique) her eyes will meet yours. There is more on the CAT below as it's great for women who are experiencing difficulty in reaching orgasm during penetration.

It takes ingenuity, trust and patient experimentation to discover positions that pleasure you both. Give and take is important when adopting sexual positions. And if lovers are truly determined to satisfy their partner's needs – being accommodating by slipping into a position that excites your lover but doesn't particularly do it for you is a truly loving gesture.

An important myth to dispel at this point is that lovers should select one position and keep to it throughout their lovemaking. *Sinful Sex* is fluid sex – not static sex! As the two of you touch and move, become more urgent or gentler and slower in pace, writhe and slip against each other, whisper and moan, your positions will almost certainly change.

This fluidity of movement is truly sensual and has been advocated by spiritual teachers dating back to the very roots of ancient Chinese thought. The Taoists, in China, believe that you achieve a spiritual connection to the universe through the interplay of the *yin* and *yang* forces – the *yin* being feminine energy, receptive and passive, and the *yang* being the masculine energy, dominant and active. Taoists believe that harmony comes from the sexual and spiritual union of a man and woman through the flow of *yin* and *yang*. Lovemaking technique is part of this flow.

Sinful positions to experience

Enjoy the freedom that communication and trust give you and allow your lovemaking to flow from one position to another. The following are just some of the many positions you can try in your lovemaking.

The CAT

I'll begin with the Coital Alignment Technique as its simplicity and effectiveness in helping a woman achieve an orgasm makes it a valuable addition to your repertoire. In this position, the woman lies *on top* – face to face – with her legs *inside* those of her lover. This squeezes the penis fairly tightly and so caution must be exercised. She then shimmies upwards an inch or two on his pelvis so that her clitoris and surrounding region will be rubbed by his pubic bone.

The movements made in the CAT, either circular or as small thrusts (or both – be creative!), allow a woman to mimic the sensations she gives herself when masturbating. The CAT is ideal as a second or third position when both lovers are aroused and perhaps the man needs slowing down while she needs now to concentrate on the right stimulation to build to orgasm. It also allows the man to rest after he has been engaged in more vigorous thrusting in other positions.

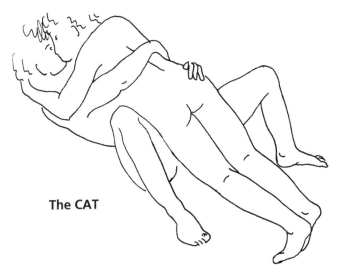

The CAT

Sinful Suggestion... Take your time and enjoy this slow sensuality as you both gaze into each other's eyes.

The Reverse Missionary

Slipping from the CAT to the Reverse Missionary is easy. The woman simply slips her thighs from between his legs and places them outside. If, for example, the extra pressure on the man's penis that the CAT provides is bringing him to orgasm too quickly, slipping into the Reverse Missionary position will relieve that. In this position, she can still stimulate her clitoris with circular motions that many women find bring them to orgasm more easily. Another variation on this theme is the Interlace. Here, the woman has one leg between his two legs, and the other leg outside. Again, such a variation is easy to slide into and provides a slightly different sensation and pressure against his penis.

Sinful Suggestion... As the woman's legs are open in the Reverse Missionary, the man can reach around to gently stroke her labia with his fingers to give her extra pleasure. From this angle he can also apply a vibrator to her anus and perineum.

The Cradle

Remaining on top, and still lying chest-to-chest, the woman can now move into the Cradle by drawing her legs up underneath her, with knees bent. This position is called the 'Cradle' because she is cradling him with her body. The Cradle is best for slow and sensual thrusting and there is the added advantage that the position allows lots of kissing. Some women find the Cradle works even better if she slips her hands under his buttocks so she can cradle him even more tightly. She can also rest her head against his shoulder.

 Sinful Suggestion... This position slightly raises the woman's bottom, allowing the man to slip his hand under her and fondle her clitoral region.

Lover's Seat

In this position, which, again, is easy to move into, the woman is sitting on top of the man. Thrusting becomes more of a slow grind unless she is quite fit and can raise herself up

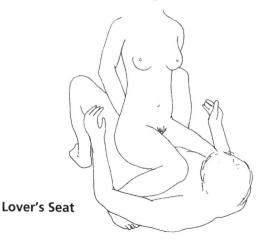

Lover's Seat

and down. Alternatively, she can do a few raises and then stop and sit to perform some slower, circular grinds while she rests her legs. The Lover's Seat allows the couple to look lovingly into each other's eyes. She may run her hands across his chest or raise herself up, perhaps to lift her hair and allow him full view of her swinging breasts.

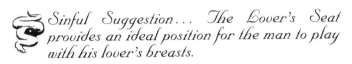

Sinful Suggestion... The Lover's Seat provides an ideal position for the man to play with his lover's breasts.

The Spinner

From the Lover's Seat, the woman can now carefully 'spin' 90 degrees to face sideways. Take care, as either of you may find this position a little uncomfortable because of the angle of the penis. However, she can then slowly 'spin' another 90 degrees so that her back is towards him. From here, she can vary the way she sits. She may lean forwards with her hands on his ankles (illustrated), or lean back placing her hands behind her (at the sides of his chest). Movement is very good as she doesn't need a lot of strength to control her thrusting. She can slip her feet underneath her (with knees bent) and, while supporting herself with her hands, raise and lower herself. This variation is known as 'offering the moon' – referring to the way the woman's bottom moves up and down in full view of the man!

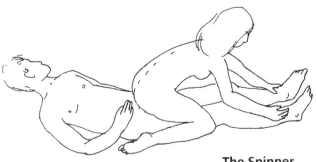

The Spinner

Sinful Suggestion… The Spinner is an excellent position for a man who loves bottoms. He can really enjoy himself caressing and stroking her buttock cheeks.

The Double Header

This is a variation on the Spinner in which the woman's back is turned to the man. Here, she shifts her weight slightly downwards as he lifts up on to his hands so that his chest is in direct skin-to-skin contact with her back.

 Sinful Suggestion… In the Double Header, the man can gently nuzzle, suck or kiss the back of her neck or shoulders as she rocks gently to and fro.

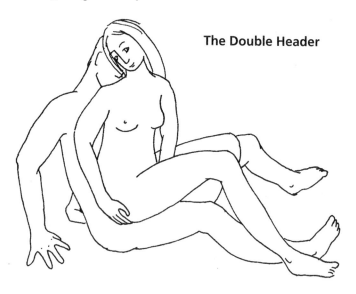

The Double Header

From the Spinner or Double Header, the man can grasp her hips and together they can slip sideways onto the bed and into the next position, the Spoons, without him withdrawing his penis.

The Spoons

This position is ideal for a lazy morning sex session or, like the CAT, to collapse into when you've been having more vigorous sex and need to quieten the pace – at least for the time being. In the Spoons, the man lies on his side, behind his lover, with the curve of her back and bottom snuggled into the curve of his body. She's on her side too and lifts her upper leg to allow him to penetrate. Some simple wriggling – usually with her pushing her bottom back and upwards a bit – ensures that he can enter her. Thrusting may then be gentle or more vigorous, depending on their mood.

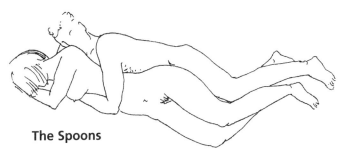

The Spoons

The Spoons is a fabulous position for allowing the man to continue foreplay. He can encircle her with his arms and run his hands up and down her erogenous zones. He can kiss and gently suck the back of her neck – a hugely pleasurable sensation, unless she's ticklish there. The Spoons feels good and if their hips are angled correctly his penis may hit her G-spot. However, without further clitoral stimulation, many women will not reach orgasm in this position – no matter how much comfort they enjoy from being cuddled by their partner.

Sinful Suggestion... In the Spoons position the man can reach around to gently stimulate her clitoral region or even the clitoris itself (whatever her preference) using his fingers or a vibrator. Or the man can encourage her to touch herself sensually as he continues his gentle thrusting.

Lover's Embrace

Here, the woman turns over so they are now facing each other, still on their sides, and can embrace. She lifts her upper thigh to allow him to penetrate. She can vary where she places her leg. She may clasp her legs together, putting extra pressure on his penis – particularly good for a man who feels he's on the small size. Or she may lift her leg higher and allow him to hold it in place. Varying the angle of her leg and hips will vary the sensations created.

Lover's Embrace

 Sinful Suggestion . . . As you embrace, let your hands wander deliciously over each other's back and bottom, cupping your lover's buttocks to keep the pressure of thrusting just right.

The Vine

From the Lover's Embrace you can slip into the Vine by interlinking your legs. Either the man or woman is slightly raised and angled on top. In this position, the two lovers' chests cross slightly allowing her breasts to rub gently against his chest.

 Sinful Suggestion . . . In the Vine, both lovers can allow their free hands to fondle their genitals during penetration.

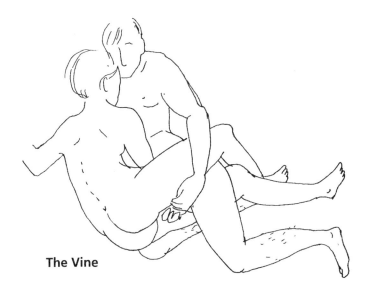

The Vine

Split the Whisker

In this position, the man crouches on his knees as the woman lies on her back – one leg resting on his shoulder. He holds her hips, thighs or knees in order to keep control and to avoid slipping out of her. They can be in bed or on the floor – whichever they choose – just so long as he can crouch comfortably. This position is fabulously erotic for allowing an intimate viewing of the vulva, which arouses so many men. And it's arousing, too, for the sexually confident woman who feels her vulva looks beautiful and seductive. This is how I want all women to feel about themselves! As two lovers gain in confidence, a woman should revel in the view she affords her man.

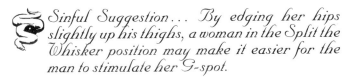

Sinful Suggestion... By edging her hips slightly up his thighs, a woman in the Split the Whisker position may make it easier for the man to stimulate her G-spot.

The Ploughman
This position is similar to Split the Whisker. The difference
lies in the woman moving her leg off the man's shoulder by
bending the knee back down so that her heel rests towards
her bottom at the side of his hip. The man, who is still
kneeling, then raises himself slightly higher, while leaning
gently against her knees and pulling her hips slightly higher
up his thighs for deep penetration.

The Ploughman

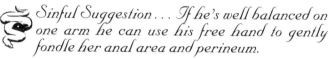

*Sinful Suggestion . . . If he's well balanced on
one arm he can use his free hand to gently
fondle her anal area and perineum.*

The Starfish
The lovers can now move into the Starfish. Here, the woman
brings both her knees towards her chest and rests her feet at
the sides of his chest or on top of his shoulders. He holds her
knees and can open them, yielding different sensations for
both lovers. The Starfish is so named because she looks like
a starfish against his kneeling posture. The woman needs to
be flexible, and the man needs a reasonable level of fitness in

order to take control of the thrusting, as his partner remains stationary in such a pose. In this position, they can clasp hands or he can lean on his arms on the bed.

 Sinful Suggestion... The Starfish is ideal for the man who likes to take control. He can thrill his lover by slowing his thrusting, deepening it, or varying the style from, say, straight thrusts to circular movements.

The Fan
This is a variation of the Starfish, but here the woman's feet are drawn in from the side of her partner's chest and pressed into his lower abdomen – like a fan folded up.

 Sinful Suggestion... The Fan is perfect for slow and sensual penetration and offers intimate eye contact.

Unfold the Flower
This position is one step on from the Starfish. Here, a supple woman can open up from the Starfish by resting the backs of her legs or knees on his shoulders. This requires great flexibility, but it also allows very deep penetration for skilled lovers.

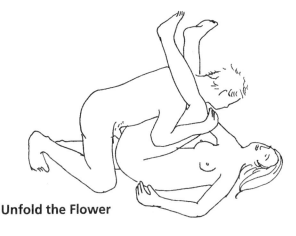

Unfold the Flower

Sinful Suggestion . . . The woman could wear a silky thong that the man slips to the side of her labia for penetration. Lots of men enjoy the sensation of a thong pulling against their thrusting.

The Crouching Tiger

Moving from Unfold the Flower into the Crouching Tiger takes skill but can be a work of art. The man, who has been kneeling, moves up onto his feet into a crouching position. He's now angled over her. She may allow her legs and feet to slip back against his chest, as in the Starfish. This counter-pressure helps control his position and thrusting.

 Sinful Suggestion . . . As he needs his hands for support she can easily reach between them to stroke the base of his penis. This area is very exposed in the Crouching Tiger.

The Lotus

Once the two lovers have tired from the Crouching Tiger they can both shift backwards so that he's sitting too. They are now

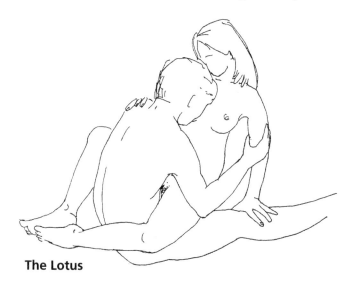

The Lotus

facing each other, with bottoms drawn together, her legs over his. He enters slowly. Vigorous thrusting isn't possible in the Lotus, but deep penetration certainly is. The Lotus is best if the woman sits slightly raised on a couple of cushions, otherwise some men may feel that their penis is being bent downwards slightly during penetration. If the lovers both gently rock together and towards each other, rather than attempt thrusting, they can create wonderful sensations. Some women find that the Lotus allows his penis to stimulate their G-spot. This position allows two lovers to look deeply into the other's eyes for a purely intimate moment. Intimacy is increased if the couple hold each other sensuously or run their fingertips and lips across each other's shoulders. Depending on the lovers' flexibility, they may be able to reach down to bring their lips to each other's nipples, in turn.

 Sinful Suggestion… In the Lotus, while gently rocking, the woman can reach round and caress her lover's buttocks and anal area to give him extra pleasure.

Easy Rider

From the Lotus it's easy to slip into the Easy Rider position. He pulls her upwards, on to his lap, so that she is sitting on him. Some of her weight is supported on her feet. He can slip more cushions behind her bottom to help support her. This will reduce the amount of downwards pressure on his penis. A gentle rocking motion will help contain his ejaculatory response while she receives the stimulation of deep penetration. The Easy Rider is great for lovemaking on a sofa or a big easy chair. While he is seated, she climbs onto him for an easy ride!

 Sinful Suggestion… In Easy Rider, the man can easily nuzzle and kiss the woman's breasts and nipples for extra stimulation. Try gentle lapping with the tongue from the base of her breasts up to her nipples — this is called the 'Naughty Dog' kiss.

The Twist

If the couple have been in the Lotus on the bed or floor they can pull away from each other into the Twist. Here, she lies back, propped up on her elbows. He slips back from underneath her and gets onto his side, twisting from the hips and with his legs either side of one of her legs. He pulls her to the point where their pubic bones touch and he can begin penetration. Great for extra friction.

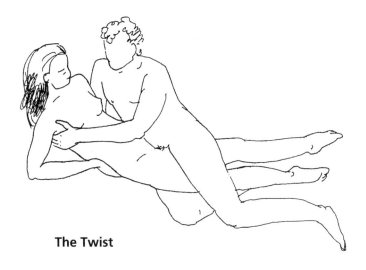

The Twist

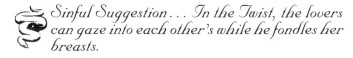

Sinful Suggestion... In the Twist, the lovers can gaze into each other's while he fondles her breasts.

Stand and Deliver

There are a number of variations on the theme of standing and facing each other. One position is for the woman to rest her back against the wall. The man then leans his hands on the wall for support or hugs the woman as he enters her. He'll need to bend his knees and angle his hips forwards in order to slip into her, unless she's taller than him so that his penis is lower than her pelvis.

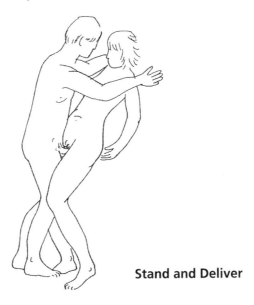

Stand and Deliver

 Sinful Suggestion... When standing, the woman could wear sexy high heels while he's barefoot. This leaves his pelvis a little lower than hers for easier penetration.

The Lift

Here, the woman rests one foot on a chair or stool while they hold on to each other. This opens her legs and lifts her pelvis slightly, allowing easier penetration for him. There's something really erotic about introducing chairs and other props into sexual positions.

The Sling

You can move into this position from the Lift, or vice versa. Standing and facing each other, the woman lifts one leg and the man 'slings' his arm underneath it to hold it in the air. Depending on her level of flexibility, he should raise or lower his arm to make this position as comfortable and pleasurable as possible for her. If she's very supple, he can raise her leg high, yielding a very open pose. She can hold onto him with one hand while using the other to stroke his or her own exposed genitals.

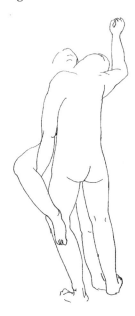

The Sling

Lover's Clasp

In this posture, he stands with his back to a wall and she wraps her legs around his and places her feet against the wall to support her. He holds her buttocks and rocks against her. This takes a lot of strength (believe me, some women find it in the name of lust). She can vary her leg position by placing one foot down on the ground, or stand on both feet, raised up on her toes (or in high heels) and leaning into him. He then uses the wall to support him as he lowers his hips in order to achieve penetration.

Strip Search

This is another variation on the standing theme. Here the woman turns her back to her lover and leans into the wall or door as he enters her from behind. If she is not taller than him and is not in high heels, he'll need to bend his knees in order to penetrate her. This position allows him to nuzzle the back of her neck – highly sensitive – and she may use one hand to fondle her clitoris. As with most positions where the man enters from behind, the Strip Search makes it easier to stimulate her G-spot.

 Sinful Suggestion… Once the couple are balanced, the man can reach around to fondle his partner's nipples.

The Puppet

A variation on the Strip Search, here the woman edges away from the wall she's been leaning on and falls forwards from the waist as if to touch the floor (like a puppet whose strings have been cut). She needs flexibility and the man must hold her hips firmly to stabilise her during his thrusting movements. This is an excellent position for a woman who likes to feel her partner's penis against her cervix.

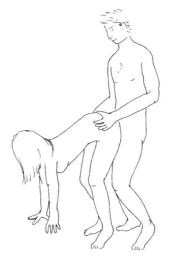

The Puppet

 Sinful Suggestion… The Puppet is great for women who like the sensation of a little gentle spanking during sex. Gently stimulate her buttocks with light slaps or smacks with one hand.

The Wheelbarrow

You can move fluidly from the Puppet into the Wheel-barrow. The woman is still bent at the waist. Now her lover picks up one or both of her legs (depending on his strength) as she rests her hands on the floor, or she may prefer to lean on her forearms. The Wheelbarrow is incredibly erotic as it opens up the woman's vulva for him to see. However, it does take strength and so the couple may wish to stay in the position for a few thrusts only before moving into another.

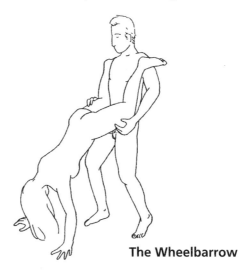

The Wheelbarrow

 Sinful Suggestion . . . Those few thrusts in the Wheelbarrow are worth it. Whisper to her how beautiful her vulva and bottom look from this angle.

Staging Post

This makes a good 'halfway house' position as you move from leaning against a wall to the bed. It's midway between Strip Search and the Doggy position. From leaning on the wall, a woman can lean on the bedstead or headboard, or kneel on the edge of the mattress. The man keeps behind her and manoeuvres his hips so that penetration may continue.

Sinful Suggestion... This slight change of position allows the man to thrust more vigorously. He can press his knees against the bed and try some 'circular' thrusts — a real treat for the G-spot from this position!

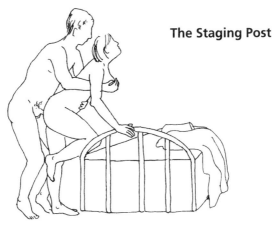

The Staging Post

Good old-fashioned Doggy

I really wish we could rename this position but everyone knows it as 'Doggy style'! She kneels on all fours on the mattress or floor. If she's pregnant or doesn't have a lot of arm strength, she should place pillows under her abdomen for support. This position is fantastic for G-spot stimulation. He can support himself on one hand and stimulate her clitoris with the other – or she can do so herself. If you have a headboard, it's easy to manoeuvre to get a slightly different feel. She lifts her hands up to grip the headboard and he follows, raising himself slightly more upright. He can grasp the headboard, too, if he wants to quicken his pace. This position is also great for a quick passion session in the sitting room. The woman kneels on the floor and leans against the sofa while he enters, Doggy style, as before. Doggy style is also good for a man who feels under-endowed. He can pull her hips firmly, tilted upwards, towards his thrusting penis. Holding her at this angle allows him to use very short but sensual strokes to give them both pleasure.

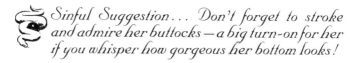

Sinful Suggestion... Don't forget to stroke and admire her buttocks – a big turn-on for her if you whisper how gorgeous her bottom looks!

The Rocking Chair

Not a position for those with weak muscles! You can move into the Rocking Chair from the Doggy or from any rear-entry position. He rests on his knees with his upper body upright. She slides her whole pelvis and hips back over his thighs – pushing her buttocks and genitals right into his pelvis. She then bends her legs so her calves grip behind his back while he reaches under and around her breasts. The couple are quite well balanced in this position so he can rock her gently. This position is ideal for women who like to yield to a man's power – as he is in complete control in this one!

The Rocking Chair

Sinful Suggestion... The Rocking Chair is superb for a slow grind or rocking motion, while he touches her clitoral region.

The Resting Dog

If either of you tire in the Doggy or Rocking Chair positions, you can easily move into the Resting Dog. Here the woman slips her hands forwards and her hips down to lie flat on her stomach. The man moves his legs flat – so that he's no longer on his knees – and rests on his hands while he carries on penetrating her from behind.

 Sinful Suggestion... She can reach around behind her, slipping her hands between her buttocks and his hips to stroke or hold the base of his penis.

The Straddle
In this position, the man is sitting on the edge of the bed. His partner straddles him, either facing him or sitting with her back to him. When facing each other, thrusting should be slow and sensual. If she has her back to him, she can use the floor to support her feet and control the pace and depth of thrusting.

The Straddle

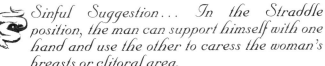 *Sinful Suggestion... In the Straddle position, the man can support himself with one hand and use the other to caress the woman's breasts or clitoral area.*

The Showman

This is not a position for novices. In the Showman, the woman kneels at the edge of the bed while he stands on the floor facing her. She arches back, thrusting her hips forwards while he controls penetration by holding her around the hips. The couple need to hold each other tightly in order to keep their balance. It may end up as a transition pose from a standing position to moving onto the bed.

 Sinful Suggestion . . . The woman can take this opportunity to confidently show off her breasts by keeping her arms above her head as he holds her tightly to maintain penetration. This will give him a welcome view of her body.

Lovers' Arch

From the Showman, the couple can move into the Lovers' Arch. She slips further back onto the bed so that he can move off the floor and get onto the bed with her. Or she can come off the bed to join him on the floor, where both kneel on a pillow. They are now facing each other while kneeling. She arches back slightly to open her pelvis, making penetration possible as he 'arches' towards her. He needs to steady them both with his strength as he slowly thrusts, allowing him to feel powerful and masculine.

 Sinful Suggestion . . . He can pull her bottom into his hips and kiss, nibble or lick her neck, which is now exposed to him.

The Rider

This position definitely requires strength on his part! In the Rider the man arches back to the floor, supporting himself on his hands. He could use a padded footstool (such as an ottoman) to support his arch. She balances one foot on the ground next to one of his feet, while slipping her other foot over his pelvis. She now begins a gentle movement along his prominently exposed penis. The Rider can be used as a gesture of simple passion, enjoying a few thrusts before moving into a less strenuous position. A variation is for the man to become the 'rider' of the woman. She arches over something for support as he stands between her legs and penetrates her, ensuring that he holds onto her hips to support her.

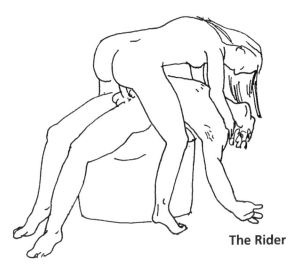

The Rider

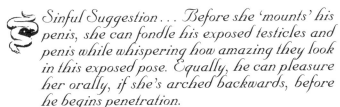

Sinful Suggestion... Before she 'mounts' his penis, she can fondle his exposed testicles and penis while whispering how amazing they look in this exposed pose. Equally, he can pleasure her orally, if she's arched backwards, before he begins penetration.

Easy Over
This is a great position for spontaneous passion that overwhelms you. The woman only needs to remove her panties and he can simply unzip his trousers. The woman moves behind an armchair or sofa and sits on the back. He clasps her hands and eases her over slowly so that her head and shoulders come to rest on the seat of the chair/sofa (supported with cushions). This means her back is arched,

leaving her hips or pelvis over the top of the chair. He holds her there and penetrates gently.

 Sinful Suggestion . . . If her head and shoulders are well supported with cushions in the seat of the chair, this position can be maintained for a while. It gives him perfect access to her clitoris — very exposed in this position.

Easy Over

The Mount
This is a variation of the Easy Over where she mounts the back of the armchair or sofa but doesn't then slump back into it. Sitting there he can begin penetration holding on to her hips or the back of the chair.

 Sinful Suggestion . . . With her free arms she can reach around and hold or caress his buttocks for pleasurable sensations.

Position '69'
This is a great position to move into for penetration, when lovers have been engaged in oral sex '69' style. As they are

already 'top to toe' the woman rolls onto her back and the man eases on top of her, supporting himself with his elbow and hands. From this position, he can gently angle his penis into her and start penetration. This position may also be initiated from the classic Missionary, with the man gently moving 90 degrees, so that he's sideways on to her, but still inside her. Then he can turn a further 90 degrees so that he's 'top to toe' with his penis still inside her. Exercise caution, as either of you may find the angle of the penis uncomfortable in this position.

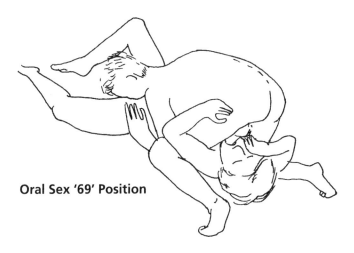

Oral Sex '69' Position

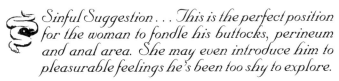

Sinful Suggestion . . . This is the perfect position for the woman to fondle his buttocks, perineum and anal area. She may even introduce him to pleasurable feelings he's been too shy to explore.

Love Knot

The more flexible the woman, the more they'll both enjoy this unusual position. The man sits in a chair or securely on the edge of a bed or sofa. The woman sits astride him wrapping her legs around him but swivels her upper body so her back faces his chest. She then reaches up and behind her, wrapping her arms around his neck – thereby forming a

Love Knot (hence the name!). The twist of her body from the waistline puts unusual pressure on penetration, yielding some fabulous sensations.

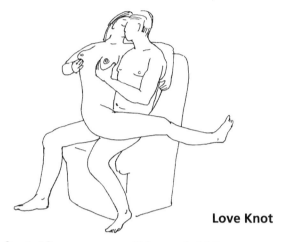

Love Knot

 Sinful Suggestion . . . He can hold her 'wrapped' arms tightly, giving a sense of 'bondage'. Or he can reach around and fondle her breasts freely or even reach down to her buttocks.

This is not an exhaustive account of the positions you and your lover could try. They would take up an entire book on their own! From these positions, though, you can be creative and allow your sexual energy to flow into other poses. Further positions that don't involve penetration – such as oral and manual sex techniques – follow in Chapters Six and Seven.

Sinful places
The importance of location is relevant for *Sinful Sex*. When we routinely make love in the same place (usually the bedroom, or a comfy old sofa) it takes the lustre off of our sex lives. Routine can start to equal boredom. Don't get me wrong – 'routine' sex, so to speak, may be comforting when

a lover is down, or one of you is feeling a bit tired. Slipping into the tried and tested place and position can be warm and snugly. But, and this is a big BUT, you don't want the location itself to dampen your ardour.

An amazing thing about humans is that we absorb our environment, particularly when arousal is heightened. All our senses take in what's available to us. And so, the same old bed, the same old bedroom furniture, the same lighting and atmosphere will be absorbed, too. Bear this in mind, particularly if you have a limited number of locations to choose from. You may need to vary the lighting, using candles or dimmers, or rearrange blankets and pillows, perhaps creating your own little 'den of lust' by piling up cushions in a corner of the room.

Sinful locations
Here are some exciting suggestions. Don't blame me if you get caught out in any of the following places. You're an adult – it's up to you where you decide to have risky encounters! Use common sense when trying somewhere daring. Depending on the location, different laws of decency may apply.

The Wonderful

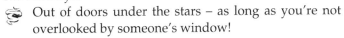 Out of doors under the stars – as long as you're not overlooked by someone's window!

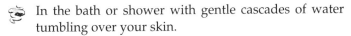 In the bath or shower with gentle cascades of water tumbling over your skin.

On the floor. It is best on carpet, or you could sling down a soft blanket and go for it on those kitchen tiles!

On your desk or workstation, the kitchen or dining table, or wherever – spontaneously as the moment takes you.

Up against the doorframe, in your front hall.

In your car, parked somewhere with a romantic view.

In the dunes at the beach, under a blanket or on top of one (sand can get into some annoying places!).

Take a walk through the forest and lean up against a big tree for support – ideal for any of the standing positions listed above.

The Wicked

In a hotel Jacuzzi late at night when the other guests aren't around.

In your office – *out of hours*.

In a friend's bathroom during a party.

On the swings in your local park, late at night.

In a swimming pool – the buoyancy makes things interesting.

On a swimming pool 'float', with the water splashing around you.

In your car in a car park.

On a deck chair at your holiday hotel at night.

In a phone box at night.

At the edges of the surf on a beach holiday with the waves gently lapping at your feet.

The Wanton

In your office – *during office hours* – hidden away in the stationery cupboard, or toilets, or behind your locked office door!

On a train or in a plane – just ensure you are discreet and don't offend anyone. If there's no suitable toilet to slip into then put a blanket over yourselves and enjoy some sinful foreplay!

In a lift while keeping the 'close doors' button pushed. Be prepared to get stuck!

Down a side street, outside the restaurant you've just dined in.

In your garden shed with the neighbours sitting innocently in their garden next door.

In the broom cupboard of a restaurant or hotel – think Boris Becker!

Sinful Suggestion . . . Ask your lover to choose one new position and combine it with a location of your choice from the list above.

6

Sinfully Delicious Oral Sex

Oral sex is a deeply intimate act that can bond two lovers in a way other techniques may not. There's something about kissing the lush and secret garden of your lover's genitals, and other erogenous zones, that's sinfully delicious. However, many men and women have reservations about oral sex. For men it's often the fear of the unknown – how do I pleasure her there? You may also worry about her taste – which is a very personal matter. Women's anxieties tend to focus on the look and taste of their own genitals (men have little anxiety about this when it comes to a woman giving them oral pleasure!) – and how to give good 'head' to a man.

By this stage you'll have more of an idea about the different parts of the genitals (if you've forgotten, go back to the illustrations in Chapter One) bearing in mind that each person is slightly different. Some men and women simply can't bring themselves to give oral sex, often because they fear the taste. Some women fear swallowing or even choking on semen. How a lover tastes (in both men and women) varies according to what they've had to eat or drink, whether they're taking medications or vitamins, and the stage a woman is at in her menstrual cycle.

Sinful Suggestion... Ask your lover to lie on the bed, slide down his clothing and gently wash his genitals with a warm, wet facecloth. This intimate gesture is highly erotic and cleanses your lover's genitals at the same time!

Getting started

It's important you talk about your feelings. Don't feel pressured into giving or receiving oral sex if you don't want to. That said, if you care for your lover (and it's not a shallow fling) and he or she would like to indulge in oral sex, look for a compromise. For example, you could simply kiss around his genitals while you fondle them with your hands. You could liberally smother her in something tasty – like chocolate sauce – that disguises her more natural taste if you're squeamish. You could perhaps pleasure him orally but not allow him to ejaculate in your mouth.

A few other considerations. Ensure your hands are clean and your nails are short when using manual techniques. Women in particular, take care with those fashionably long nails on his tender foreskin, glans, testicles and perineum.

Let's begin at the beginning – hygiene! Unless your lover has a fetish for sweaty genitals, you both need to be aware of your hygiene. Showering or bathing together first is a good idea – it will not only kick off your sex play but also leave you smelling and tasting fresh, too. Otherwise, washing in preparation for oral delights offers a good opportunity to treasure yourself and build up the anticipation of oral sex to come. Be aware, though, that some people are sensitive to douching or some types of soap. This can lead to genital irritation that, ironically, causes a smell. So don't overdo it with soaps and shower gels. In addition, there are various infections that need treatment and which can cause genital odours – if in doubt see your doctor.

In giving oral sex, you'll notice that the female genitals change in appearance during sexual arousal (as, of course, does the penis when it becomes erect). The labia 'blush' a deeper red and become more swollen as they engorge with blood. The clitoris expands and rises up from under the clitoral hood – although just before climax it retracts again. Noticing these changes gives you a big clue that you're on the right track. But never forget that a woman needs fairly constant stimulation – the way she likes it – to bring these changes to their natural climax.

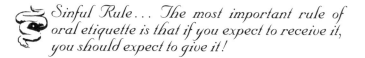

Sinful Rule… The most important rule of oral etiquette is that if you expect to receive it, you should expect to give it!

Giving sinfully delicious oral pleasure to her
I can't stress this enough – and as you should already know from previous chapters – ask what sort of oral sex your lover likes. The different oral techniques use the lips and/or the tongue (and even the teeth, in delicate genital 'biting'). A woman may prefer a man to start by using his lips only as her clitoris is quite sensitive to little jabs of the tongue. He could kiss her genitals as he would her lips. She may then like him to use his tongue for a stronger sensation as she builds to orgasm, or she might prefer him to continue with his lips, but closing them, rather than puckering, and using them in a circular 'grinding' motion. Without asking, you won't find out!

A good way to start (after you've been enjoying lots of manual foreplay across her erogenous zones!) is to ask if you can watch her touch herself – a fantastically erotic learning experience. Make sure you are comfortable before using one of the positions for oral sex described below. Run your tongue and lips from her lower abdomen, across her pubic bone and then down her labia towards her vaginal opening, covering the entire area. Let her guide you to repeat certain sensations – or not, as the case may be. Even though you've asked for guidance at the start, ask her again occasionally if it still feels good. Encourage her to cradle your head with her hands to help keep you on course.

Positions for giving oral sex

The man needs to find a comfortable position as his lover may need twenty minutes – or more – of oral sex to reach climax. Comfort is, of course, equally important for women when they give oral sex to a man, even though men don't usually take so long to climax. Feel free to shift between positions occasionally so that you stay comfortable.

Full On

In this position, she lies back and you lie between her legs. She can then spread her legs or place one or both of her legs over your shoulders. Both of you may use your hands to open her labia as much as she likes. You can also use your thumbs to gently spread her labia in this position. And she can easily hold and guide your head. Full On is best for lip and tongue action alone, rather than inserting your finger as well.

Hard to Get

Here, your lover keeps her thighs together so you can approach from below, moving up and over her closed thighs. This is a good position for the woman who's very sensitive to touch. It keeps her clitoris tucked away. If she gets very aroused by your kissing she can, of course, open her thighs.

Across the Bridge

You are sideways on to her hips in this position, and she has her legs apart. Place one of your hands on her pubic bone, and gently pull upwards on her lower abdomen to expose her clitoris. This is great position for you because you can use the hand resting between her legs for some fingering – which we'll cover further on. With your tongue, gently lap sideways across her clitoris to give her an incredibly erotic sensation.

Down Under

In this position you come to her from above, so your legs are near her head, to rest on her abdomen. This allows you to lick downwards gently across her clitoris, creating new sensations – again great for the extra-sensitive woman. You can also reach down with your tongue to stroke her labia, or go even further to stimulate her perineum 'Down Under'.

Raising the Flower
This is a good position for supple lovers. She lies on her back while you kneel between her legs. She places her calves on your shoulders and you rise up slightly, bringing her hips off the bed and her genitals to your mouth. You then steady her with one hand wrapped around her waist – and the other can play with her breasts. Raising the Flower is great for the woman who loves to show off her 'flower' – as you get a full view!

Worship the Triangle
She lies on her stomach with her pelvis arched slightly upwards or on her side with her legs open. You come to her from behind – towards the 'triangle' that's formed by her thighs and buttocks. It allows you to kiss the sensitive areas of her lower labia, buttocks, perineum and anus (don't forget safer sex here – use a dental dam or cling film!). Again, this position is good for a woman with a very sensitive clitoris.

Sitting Pretty
She sits on the edge of the bed, chair or sofa and spreads her legs. You kneel between them to gain easy access to her genitals. She can really guide your head in this position. It's quite an erotic feeling for the woman to have a man at her feet as he's serving her almost like a sex-slave. Don't forget – for some spontaneous sex in the kitchen or bathroom you can hoist her onto a counter top for easy access!

Easy Over
Adapting this position for penetrative sex in Chapter Five, the woman sits on the back of an armchair or sofa and allows her head and back to slip down into the seat. This exposes

her genitals for a real 'feast'. A really daring position that can be exhilarating for both lovers.

Standing Pleasure

Here, she stands with her legs apart and you kneel below her. You can then lift upwards to kiss her genitals. She should stand near a wall or chair to steady her – just in case she gets carried away by the sensations. This is a great one to try in the shower, particularly for a man who is concerned about how she may taste. As the water cascades gently around them, continually washing her, he laps at her genitals.

'69'

This position allows you to pleasure each other at the same time. Either one of you lies on your back and the other kneels on top – head to toe. Both of you can give oral pleasure in this position. The sight of your lover's genitals just above or below your face can be extremely arousing – and it provides good access for perineum-play!

Lover's Knot

This is simply '69' while lying on your side, head to toe. Again, you can pleasure each other at the same time. You may find you can stay in the Lover's Knot for longer than in the traditional '69'. It's easier for both of you to hug and fondle the other this way, too. In '69' the person on top needs to use an arm for support, making it more difficult to add manual pleasure to oral stimulation.

Reach the Peach

You lie on your back and your lover kneels above you, offering herself to be orally pleasured. She can tease and tempt you by raising herself up on her knees just out of reach of your lips. Once she wants to be brought to climax, you can hold her and draw her to your lips by looping your arms under her buttocks and holding her tightly.

Sinful Suggestion... Depending on the position you choose, feel free to use cushions to raise her hips for better 'feasting' or place them under your chest to give you support.

Mouth magic
An excellent way to get to grips with sinfully delicious oral sex is to think of it as dining on a *pleasurable feast*. The following will create different sensations.

Licking
Use your tongue gently at first. Think of how you'd lick an ice-cream cone delicately. You can try upwards strokes with your tongue on her outer and inner labia, her vaginal opening and clitoral region.

Lapping
A bigger and more earthy version of licking. Let your mouth hang open, completely relax your tongue and use larger lapping movements from her perineum up to her vagina and over her labia. If she's very sensitive, this will also feel great across her pubic bone.

Poking
For inserting your tongue into her vagina, pretend that you're gently poking it into a soft and delicate sponge cake. She may also like the poking sensation down her clitoral arms – either side of her clitoris – down along the sides of her labia. Gentle poking feels sensational on the perineum and anus. (Just play safe by using plastic dams or cling film. You don't want to pick up any of the bacteria from her anus – or transfer anything to her vagina.)

Swirling
Think of a gorgeously gentle whirlpool and then try that with your tongue by swirling gently around her clitoral area. Don't touch the clitoris directly – unless she likes it!

Sucking

Imagine how you'd gently suck in a long piece of spaghetti. Apply this sucking sensation to her clitoris – when she's ready – or to her inner labia, sucking one part for a moment and then gently moving on down her labia.

Kissing

Always start with soft kisses, asking her for guidance before building up to a firmer kiss. As with mouth kissing, relaxed lips are more sensual. If her clitoris is highly sensitive, or if she takes a long time to build to climax, she may like you to place your lips around her clitoris and simply pulse them gently. She can hold your head and grind herself more firmly against your lips as she builds to climax.

Rubbing

Again, using the lips, instead of a kissing action, you rub gently back and forth or around and around with your lips against her clitoral area and down across her labia.

Flicking

A very gentle flicking motion up and down her labia and perineum can feel fabulous. But beware of 'flicking' her clitoris with your tongue – most women don't like this sensation (although you won't know if she's one of the few who do unless you ask!) Too many porn films show men (and other women) flicking away at the clitoris – but most women simply can't take this.

Humming

I've been saving the most sinful for last! Try humming when your lips are wrapped gently around her labia! The gentle vibrations are incredibly erotic.

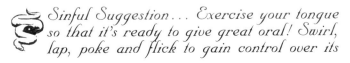

Sinful Suggestion ... Exercise your tongue so that it's ready to give great oral! Swirl, lap, poke and flick to gain control over its

movement. (Practise in secret — your new-found expertise will be a great surprise for her!)

Direct clitoral stimulation

If she enjoys direct clitoral stimulation (ask first, or she may jump out of her skin!) place your hand flat across her pubic bone and slide it gently upwards about 1cm (about ½in). This will lift her clitoral hood (prepuce) and expose her clitoris. Alternatively, if you are sideways on to her (as in Across the Bridge) place your thumb and forefinger on either side of her clitoris, on her outer labia, and again gently raise the clitoral hood by pulling upwards.

If she's one of the majority of women who don't enjoy such direct stimulation, ensure her hood stays in place until engorgement pushes her clitoris out from underneath. Women who have a larger hood may find the clitoris never 'peeps' out during arousal.

 Sinful Suggestion... Some people are uncomfortable with the formal names for the genitals. If so, give each other's sex organs erotic nicknames. For example, you may name her clitoris her 'Love-bud' and she may name your penis 'Captain Sex'. Then when asking what sort of sensation your lover wants you can say things like, 'Would Love-bud like some tongue-licking or lip-kissing?' Men — beware — some women find words such as 'muff-diving' offensive. So use such slang with caution.

Fingering techniques to use with oral sex

As described in Chapter Four, you can use your fingers in all sorts of ways. So be inventive and adapt my suggestions for fingering as you continue to kiss, lick and suck her with your lips and tongue for a total oral experience.

Twirling

Use both fingers together, as if you were twirling a piece of string. Apply the twirling to just around the clitoris – NOT on the clitoris itself! Done very gently to the surrounding area, this can perfectly stimulate the clitoris.

Stroking

Otherwise known as 'stroking the mouse's nose', here you use your index and middle fingers to gently caress the clitoral hood and arms, the labia, vaginal opening, perineum and anus. Remember, if you touch her anus, wash your hands before touching her genitals again, or you can spread germs.

Drumming

Some women love a light 'drumming' sensation across their pubic bone, down their clitoral arms and along their labia. Do it delicately – imagine your fingertips are gentle raindrops.

Rubbing

A subtle version of Stroking, imagine gently 'sanding' with your index and middle fingers. This is a small back-and-forth movement that's very delicate!

Circular massage

Taking the outer labia between the thumb, index and middle fingers, apply a circular, delicate massaging motion. Done sensually, it'll bring blood rushing to the labia to engorge them.

Finger positions

To put to sinful use the various types of genital fondling described, here are some finger positions to try on women. Don't forget to apply vaginal lubricants regularly to help her along.

The 'V' sign!
You have already met this in Chapter Four. It is great for initial stimulation before you give oral sex, or it can be applied while you stimulate her with your tongue and lips in the Across the Bridge position. As she becomes moist, move the 'V' sign formed by your index and middle fingers 'southwards', allowing one finger to slip inside her vagina.

The Full Four
Allow all four of your fingers to relax down and over her pubic bone in a 'cupping' position with your fingertips touching her vagina. From this position you can do the Stroking, Rubbing or Circular Massage motions. When she's nice and lubricated, you can slip, one, two or three fingers into her vagina.

The Beak
Bring your fingertips and thumb together to form a beak. Your hand should be turned palm upwards while applying the beak. Once she's very lubricated, you can use a gentle circular massage with your beak on her vagina and into her vaginal opening, at the same time giving oral pleasure around her clitoris. Watch those nails!

Labial Massage
While she is lying with her legs open, crouch above her and use all your fingers and thumbs to work your way gently down one side of her outer labia and up the other – then gently circle her clitoris. Imagine you are *delicately* kneading some delicious bread dough – not unlike 'twirling' it very gently between your fingers and thumbs. Keep it delicate and ensure your fingers are lightly coated in lubricant for her pleasure. Don't pull on her labia!

The Handful
This is an excellent technique to use when she's highly aroused, again with her legs open and you kneeling.

Keeping your fingers together and your hands lightly cupped, gently alternate moving your left and right hand up and down from her pubic bone down over her labia and inner thighs. Use large, but delicate, sweeping motions with the hands, passing each other in opposite directions as they move up and down over her genitals. This technique can build intimacy as the woman is completely exposed to the loving touch of the man.

Loving the Pearl
Once she's well stimulated, use this technique if she'd like more direct clitoral massage. Rest your thumb and index finger on either side of her clitoris, either with the hood pulled up or not – whichever she prefers. Gently rub her clitoris back and forth with small motions between the thumb and index finger. Start slowly and build the pace, checking with her how it feels.

Rear Pleasure
This is ideal for the man with a fascination for his lover's bottom. While kneeling on the floor, she bends over the sofa or bed-edge while you stroke her from behind. This is perfect for kissing her buttocks and anal area, and (as in Worshipping the Triangle) for kissing her labia and vagina, if she arches her pelvis towards you slightly. While kneeling behind her, with your hand opened as if to shake hands, you can hold her perineum and labial area, gently rocking your cupped hand in a back-and-forth or circular motion (or both).

The Stir
Using your index and middle fingers held together, insert them into her vagina slowly, and make a 'stirring' motion with them. Gently stir them around and around to carefully stimulate her vaginal walls.

The Grip
Making a 'C' shape with your thumb and four fingers, insert your thumb into her vagina, leaving your four fingers across

her clitoral region. You can then gently rotate your thumb inside her. Alternatively, using this gentle 'grip', move your whole hand back and forth gently so that she gets vaginal and clitoral stimulation.

Come On Over

This is perfect for stimulating her G-spot as you kiss her clitoral region. Imagine your index and middle fingers, palm upwards, making a 'come on over' gesture. When inserted into her vagina, your fingers should reach her G-spot, up about 5cm (around 2in) on the front (tummy) wall of her vagina. For a double whammy – try a gentle stroking motion against her G-spot as you pleasure her clitoris with your lips and tongue! More on G-spot stimulation in Chapter Seven.

> *Sinful Suggestion... When giving oral pleasure, you can also do what I call 'nose nuzzling' – before, during or after you apply your lips and tongues. Simply use the tip of your nose to nuzzle her genitals – the intimacy will heighten her pleasure.*

A word of warning

Everyone's heard of the infamous Mars Bar 'incident' where a famous rock star is said to have shared one with a singer in a rather unorthodox way. Over the years, women's vaginas have undoubtedly played 'hostess' to chocolates of all shapes and sizes that their lovers have feasted on. This can be sticky, fun and tasty.

However, when it comes to other items lurking in your household that may be inserted into your lover, you should exercise great care. Obviously I'm not talking here about sex toys designed to be inserted into the vagina or rectum (see Chapter Nine for more on those), but unsuitable items such as wine bottles (never insert anything made of glass), the ends of hairbrushes, spoons, cucumbers, carrots and shampoo bottles. Virtually anything people could get their hands on have been used as makeshift dildos. The problem is, you never know if these items may break, be covered in germs, or generally have an unpleasant after-effect. Even the innocent bar of soap can irritate the delicate pH balance of the vagina or rectum – causing loads of discomfort. So apart from the innocent bit of chocolate (or other sauces, mentioned in Chapter Four), without being a killjoy, stick to the purpose-made items intended for this type of sex play. To liven things up as you are moving a delicately vibrating sex toy in and out of your lover's vagina, don't forget to use your tongue and lips on her, too!

 Sinful Secret . . . Only about the first third of a woman's vagina is really sensitive. So, if she doesn't respond enthusiastically when you push your fingers further up inside her, it doesn't mean there is anything wrong with her! That said, many women enjoy the sensation of their cervix (located at the end of the vagina) being 'bumped' during thrusting, either with the penis or a vibrator. But take care, some women find this painful.

Biting and nibbling
Time for a warning! Some people love the feeling of being 'nibbled' – and a skilled lover will do this well. It can feel deliciously erotic to alternate licking and kissing with gentle biting. However, if you are going to nibble or 'bite' your lover, particularly in the genital region, you need to exercise considerable care. This is particularly important if you've been drinking (excess alcohol can lead to poor quality sex) as you don't want to get carried away and damage your lover's delicate skin. Human bites are full of germs!

For a little sinful nibbling, you could keep to the skin of the inner thigh, lower abdomen or buttocks, rather than biting the genitals. Other sites for little bites include the area behind the knees, encircling the ankles and the back of the neck.

Giving sinfully delicious oral pleasure to him

This section on giving oral pleasure to men is much briefer than the women's section. Men's oral pleasure isn't any less important – definitely not! But if you've taken on board the information above on oral sex for her (and I hope women readers were paying attention – it's your pleasure I was describing!) then you're already a long way to being able to give a man sinfully delicious oral sex. You can use most of the tongue and lip activities on a man, as well as some of the hand and finger techniques. Use your imagination! Here are a few extras to fill in the gaps when giving oral pleasure to a man:

Special oral techniques to use on him

Start slowly on a man and ask as you go – just as he should ask you. Again, he may be happy to touch himself while you watch so you get a sense of what he likes. While working your way down his abdomen with playful licks and kisses, your hands can be snaking across his pelvis and around between his thighs. He will love being stimulated by your hands and mouth at the same time – just as a woman loves both sensations. Even if you simply stroke his testicles while you concentrate on what your mouth is doing – that's an added bonus.

Foreskin

Just as a man should be careful not to pull back the clitoral hood without checking whether she likes that – so, too, must a woman go easy when pulling back the foreskin in a non-circumcised man. Ask him to show you how he pulls it back – he may use a firm movement or be more gentle. If he likes, you can then hold it down at the base of his glans. However, all men are different – some may prefer a woman to grip the shaft, the base, or nearer the tip of the glans.

Testicles, perineum and anal area
Many men are too shy to admit that they like these areas to
be stimulated. You need to take the lead by letting him know
you want him to enjoy some sinful stimulation. Make sure
he's fresh and clean, and then you can safely lick and kiss his
testicles and perineum, covering the anal area with cling
film or a dental dam to stop transmission of germs, if you'd
like to orally pleasure him there. Straight men can learn a lot
from gay men here!

Some men prefer simple stimulation – rather than loads of
kissing, licking and lapping. Try holding his testicles in your
hand while giving him oral sex. From there you may
alternate between gently pulling and then releasing the
testicles. He may prefer his perineum massaged very gently,
particularly if he's never indulged in such pleasures, as he
may be very sensitive there.

Positions to use for pleasuring him
As previously described, you may like to lie between his
legs, to the sides of his legs, or (as in Across the Bridge) lie at
right angles to him. Here are a few other suggestions.

Worshipping at the Altar
He stands on the floor while you kneel between his legs. This
is great for a man who likes his buttocks caressed during oral
sex as you can reach up and under his perineum or around
his hips to grip them.

Kneeling Pose
Here, you lie flat on your back while he kneels over your
chest. He then lowers his pelvis so you can reach his penis
with your mouth and his testicles with your hands. You can
also control his movements by gripping his buttocks.

Picking the Plums
In this position, he kneels, resting back slightly on his legs
and leaving his penis and testicles dangling a foot or so

above the bed. You lie on your stomach and arch up to lick his testicles or penis. Or you can lie on your back, with your head between his thighs. You can then use your hand on his penis while you stimulate his testicles with your mouth.

Oral techniques to try
Having always asked the expert (him!) first, try the following.

Sucking
Suck on his glans as if it were a lollipop. Simply ensure you use the pressure he desires and don't get carried away like a vacuum pump!

Licking
Lick him as if he is an ice-cream cone – from the base of his shaft up towards the glans. Really lube him up with your saliva so your tongue slips up and down easily. If you like some of the edible, flavoured lubricants on the market, slather it on!

Fluttering
Try fluttering your tongue like a butterfly's wing. Fluttering up and down his shaft, alternating with whole, long sucks, will feel sensational.

Special sensations
As for women, swirling, kissing, humming, rubbing and lapping are sensations he will love.

Poking
Some men love to feel the tip of the tongue gently poking in and out of their urethra. So ask! Otherwise you may gently 'poke' his perineum, running up and down it and, at intervals, pausing to apply a little pressure. Men often have one particular place in this area where pressure feels particularly good, so try to locate it by asking him to tell you where your poking feels best.

Holding

Simply holding his testicles in your mouth while you move your fingers up and down his shaft gives some men great pleasure. This is a good time to try a little humming, too!

The Suction

At some point during stimulation, most men like a little suction applied with the mouth to bring them to orgasm. I say 'most men' as some very sensitive men don't enjoy this sort of stimulation. Slip the whole of his glans into your mouth and form a suction with your lips and inner mouth. Depending on what he likes, you could circle or lap with your tongue, or gently suck his glans while using the suction. Experiment to see what he loves most.

 Sinful Suggestion... Some men and women love the tingling sensation that comes from sucking a mint or a little toothpaste, or a piece of citrus fruit such as lemon or lime, and then giving oral sex.

Manual techniques

Men vary in how they like to be held when you're focussing on stimulating the glans and upper shaft. Your lover may like a firm grip with your entire hand wrapped around the base of his shaft. Alternatively, he may prefer to feel your thumb and forefinger ringed around his penis. Again, ask if you can watch his technique – definitely the best way to learn!

Basic Hold

Ensure your hands are well lubricated with an edible lubricant as you slide your hand up and down. He may like you to alternate the pressure you apply as well as alternating with any of the following finger techniques. Or you could add to the Basic Hold with some rhythmic massage, drumming, fluttering or swirling your fingers up and down his shaft and around his glans.

The Juicer
Kneeling beside him, hold the base of his shaft with one hand and his glans with the other as if about to juice an orange. Then gently rotate that hand back and forth – ensure you've got plenty of lubricant on your hand! Let him guide you as you build up speed on this move.

The Double-header
As you suck, lick and flutter your tongue over his glans, wrap your left thumb and forefinger around the base of his shaft and your right thumb and forefinger above them. Start by moving them up and down together. Then separate them and starting mid-shaft, move them in opposite directions – the right moving up while the left moves down. Then move them back towards each other. Repeat these two variations.

Some important considerations
Here are some more points to bear in mind when giving your lover oral sex.

Building to orgasm
Men usually climax through oral sex more quickly than women. However, it can take longer if they've consumed alcohol or taken medication, or if they're feeling anxious or unwell in any way. Once he's been driven a bit mad with a sinful variety of touches and licks, he'll need you to maintain a constant rhythm, usually with the Basic Hold, often building in frequency and pressure until he climaxes. Get to know what he likes and then use oral sex to help him learn to control his orgasm – so that he may last longer during penetrative sex. This is a good enough reason for anyone who thinks she won't like giving oral sex to give it a whirl!

Swallowing semen
This is a very individual choice. If you feel you would rather

not, there are ways around it. Never feel you have to swallow – he can still enjoy oral pleasure without this. And, of course, there are safer sex considerations.

Deep throating
Some men have a notion – usually gleaned from porn films – that deep throating is highly erotic. For most women, the gag reflex simply won't allow them to do it and they don't like the sensation of being 'choked'. If you are willing to try, you need to be in a position where your head is held back and your throat is in line with your mouth. This provides a straight passage and avoids the sensation that the penis has to bend around into your throat. It's a very individual thing. Don't, whatever you do, practise with bananas, as some women claim to have done. A banana can break off in your throat and choke you – seriously dangerous!

Body and facial hair
Some men love the idea of 'shaven-havens' as it gives them better access to your delicate pleasure zones. Some women also like their partners' genitals to be shaved – particularly as some men have masses of pubic hair to get through. Again, this is highly individual. You should have some fun talking it through without offending your lover. If you don't want the hassle of shaving completely, women can opt for a 'Brazilian' style wax that leaves the hair nearest the labia but strips the rest. Alternatively, try a 'landing strip', which leaves a nice straight strip along the lower pelvis. Men may agree to be neatly trimmed or simply shave around their testicles. However, if your lover doesn't want to trim or shave, before you start giving oral sex, run your fingers through the pubic hair to get rid of any loose hairs that may become trapped in your teeth or throat.

Sinful Suggestion... You can take turns shaving and trimming each other's pubic hair in a sensual way. Stroke your fingers through their hair as you are trimming them. Admire the beauty of their genitals and they'll feel very aroused.

Men with facial hair often don't realise how unpleasant this can feel when kissing. A beard or moustache that feels soft and silky to you can irritate a woman's very delicate genitals! To check, gently rub your facial hair on her inner thigh and ask how it feels before proceeding further.

 Sinful Suggestion... Try exchanging some oral juices! The man sucks gently on your vagina — getting some of your juices in his mouth. Then he kisses your mouth, slipping some of your juices into it. Incredibly erotic. You may also allow him to taste himself but men, being the tender creatures they are, are less likely to want to try this!

Safer and sinful oral sex

As you know, I gave a general warning at the beginning of the book – it's your responsibility to ensure you protect your sexual health. Considering the sinful suggestion I've just made, this is a good moment to repeat it. If there are any doubts about your partner's sexual health, it is possible to give a man oral sex while he wears a condom. Why do you think flavoured condoms became available? Be careful not to rupture it with your teeth, though! The same is true for a woman – placing a dental dam or good-quality cling film over her vagina barely detracts from the sensation of oral sex and yet will protect you from transmission of infections – as long as you don't rupture the barrier.

Enjoy the wonderfully sensuous experience of oral sex. The men reading this should know that the key to a woman's heart is held by the lover who relishes giving good oral sex. The depth of intimacy attained through these techniques will bring you both to deeper levels of sinfully erotic sex.

7

More Sinful Suggestions

Now that you know how to communicate with your lover about indulging in sinful foreplay, oral sex and getting creative with sexual positions, it's time to *fine-tune* your lovemaking skills. Don't forget that your personal attitude plays an important part in this – the more confident you are about expressing yourself sexually, the more imagination you can put into these suggestions!

Sinful touching suggestions

Here are some sinful suggestions for you to embrace and experiment with.

Feathering

Drizzle any massage/scented oil you like down your lover's breasts, back, thighs and abdomen – in fact, anywhere they like. Taking a commercially prepared feather (that's clean!) swirl it gently through the oil. For example, if you've drizzled oil down your lover's breasts you may take the feather and move it around the base of her breasts – gathering some of the oil on its tip. Now draw the oily tip up the breast to the nipple, flicking the end of it. She'll relish the wonderful sensations of feathering – and so will you.

Erotic brushing

This follows a similar principle to feathering. Using a kitchen basting brush (again, clean!) or artist's brush, gently swirl sensual oil, cream or chocolate sauce over your lover's body. You can then lick off any edible sauces used! For sheer ecstasy, try gently brushing between the buttocks. You could also number your body with a brush and chocolate sauce and ask your lover to follow the numbers.

Balloon Play

This feels fabulous on sensitive skin. Blow up a balloon (you could keep a few in your Foreplay Treasure Chest – see page 45) but don't tie a knot in it. Controlling the release of air carefully with your fingertips, allow the air to trace a path over your lover's naked skin. Begin at her lips and move the airflow over her chest, down her abdomen and over her inner thighs. (But don't allow the air to blow up inside her vagina, owing to the danger of air bubbles.) Then she can do the same to you.

Ice Play

On a steamy summer evening – or when you've got things nicely steamed up in chillier times – take an ice cube and gently trace a sensuous path down your lover's body. Another way is to take the cube between your lips and draw it over the body. Alternate the cold of the ice with the warmth of your tongue, lapping up the little droplets of melted water. On a very hot day, the labia respond well to having ice traced around them. Now try nibbling the slightly numbed area very gently with your teeth.

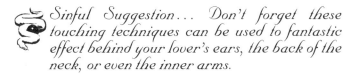 *Sinful Suggestion... Don't forget these touching techniques can be used to fantastic effect behind your lover's ears, the back of the neck, or even the inner arms.*

Wax Play

A famous singer is said to relish a bit of Wax Play and, like Ice Play, it heightens the sensitivity of the skin in preparation for other pleasures. Use a good quality wax and test the droplets on the inside of your wrist to ensure they're not too hot. Dropping little droplets of wax from the height of about 1m (3ft) lets them cool enough not to hurt the skin.

Warning

Many people enjoy Wax Play but you **can** get burnt – so don't try this unless you trust your lover implicitly. It's not a technique for someone with delicate skin. Have a cool wet cloth handy in case your lover finds the droplets are too hot and beware of small pieces of burning wax dropping onto the skin. **You have been warned – this is your responsibility!**

Extra manual suggestions

Here are some more suggestions to spice up your sex play.

The Snake

When a man is manually stimulating his lover's vagina he could try the Snake. Ensuring that she is well lubricated, and after having manually stimulated her with two fingers, he uses the two fingers together, slightly curved upwards, and gently wiggles them from side to side to apply a gentle, jiggling pressure to her vaginal walls. The Snake feels like a vibrator in slow motion!

Changing of the Guard

People forget that by constantly using their preferred hand – right or left – to stimulate their lover's genitals manually they are neglecting an easily available alternative sensation. Simply change hands and it will feel very different on his penis, testicles and perineum, and her clitoral region, labia, vagina and perineum.

Veiled Touch

An interesting twist with 'fetish' undertones is to slide on a pair of soft gloves – preferably of a velvety texture (and make sure they are clean so your lover doesn't get any irritation). Now gently caress your lover's erogenous zones for a touch with a difference.

The Whole Palm
When adding a lubricant to manual sex play, a man can use his whole palm to gently rub his lover's pubis, clitoral region, vagina and along her perineum. If, while he uses this technique, he holds her thighs apart with his other hand she'll feel completely under his control.

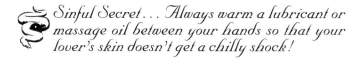

Sinful Secret . . . Always warm a lubricant or massage oil between your hands so that your lover's skin doesn't get a chilly shock!

Silken Scarf or Panty Play…
As mentioned in Chapter One, running a silky scarf across the genitals or other part of the body can heighten sensitivity. She can roll on her side and spread her legs while he pulls the scarf back and forth across her labia and clitoris. The best way to do this is if he holds his hands on either side of her body as he runs the scarf from her pubic bone, along her labia, and up over her buttocks. Using the same method, she can rub the scarf against his testicles and perineum. Instead of a scarf, use silky panties, sliding them across her nipples, down to her genitals, and over her buttocks. For a little 'gender bending' she can slip the panties on to the man and then stroke him through the silky fabric.

Keep that silky scarf handy for some teasing strip-play. Standing in front of your lover – as scantily clad as you like – sway your hips as you pull the silky cloth between your thighs or run it over your breasts, teasing your nipples so that they become erect.

Stripping
This brings me conveniently to the erotic enjoyment you can both get from stripping. Women love it when men strip for

them, too. Practise on your own with the kind of music you feel good moving to – it may be a thumping rock beat or a smooth R & B number. You'll build confidence by wearing clothing you feel sexy in and that are easy items to remove (no complicated buttons or hooks). Both men and women should sway their hips from side to side and then try some pelvic thrusts. Use your imagination and pretend you're a lap dancer or a male stripper. Visualise the sorts of moves they do and add them to your repertoire. Touch and fondle yourself and think about the things you'd say if your lover was watching you.

When it is time to perform in front of your lover, dim the lights or use candles, put on an audio tape or CD, push your partner into a chair and start your strip – slow, sensual and teasing. You might even bind your lover's hands to the chair so there's no touching. She can push his head between her breasts – he can swing his penis in front of her eyes. You can fondle, touch and tease your lover but your partner can't touch you! And don't forget, you can both do some 'research' for your strip routines by going together to watch professional strippers. Couples often find it a huge turn-on to watch top strippers in action. Women can join a strip class to build body confidence. Unfortunately, there don't seem to be any classes available for men yet.

G-spot stimulation

Having mentioned the Come On Over technique in Chapter Six, let's take a look at the G-spot generally. You can stimulate the G-spot using oral, manual or penetrative techniques. The first thing two lovers should do is explore the woman in delicious detail to see if she has a sensitive G-spot.

Some studies show that about 70 per cent of women claim to have this extra G-spot sensitivity on the front inner wall of their vagina. They often notice it most with rear-entry positions such as Spoons or Doggy style when the penis is thrusting against the front wall of the vagina. However, if a woman does not recognise such sensitivity, it does not mean that she is any less of a woman, or less sexy, or going to enjoy sex less than a woman who is highly sensitive there. A woman can still have mind-blowing orgasms so it doesn't matter a jot whether they arise from the G-spot! I don't want anyone to get a complex from reading *Sinful Sex* – instead I want you to be open to possibilities.

The best way to explore her G-spot sensitivity is, quite frankly, whichever way she prefers! Once she's aroused and lubricated she may like you to try the Come On Over finger position or use a dildo or vibrator for a gentle poke around. You could, of course, try a nice slow session of Spoons. As you slowly 'massage' her internally with your penis, ask about the different sensations she's experiencing. One way to bring a woman to the heights of sexual tension is by teasing her with some very slow circular thrusting from behind – so these are ideal for your G-spot investigations.

You could introduce a little fantasy play into this exploratory session. Pretend you're a massage expert and you two felt 'lust at first sight' when she booked an appointment with you. As you'll see in Chapter Eight, such chat can free you from inhibitions.

How best to stimulate her G-spot during penetrative sex mainly depends on the shape of your penis. Men with a very straight penis will find that the Doggy or Spoons position works very well. However, if your penis curves towards your stomach, you may find those positions in which you face each other do the trick. This is particularly true with positions such as Unfold the Flower (Chapter Five), where your curvature will hit her front vaginal wall naturally.

The U-Spot

Some women swear by a little place called the U-spot – saying it's more exciting then their G-spot. This is the little area of delicate skin located just above the opening of the urethral canal, roughly 0.5cm (about ¼in) below the clitoris. The urethral opening itself is just above the opening to the vagina. Lightly touching or 'rubbing' this little spot (with the finger, tongue or nose even!) has been likened to rubbing the genie's magic lamp! Some sex researchers think pressure here might lead to a build-up of secretions in the peri-urethral glands inside the vagina. And it may be associated with the elusive female ejaculation. Again, this gives you the perfect excuse (and who needs one?) for some fantasy play. You two can be sexy scientists who need to proceed carefully with a detailed examination of this area to find out if this or the surrounding pleasure centres truly excite her! Be very careful when stimulating this intimate spot as over-stimulation may lead to irritation of the urethral canal.

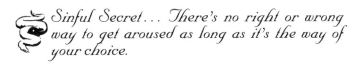 *Sinful Secret… There's no right or wrong way to get aroused as long as it's the way of your choice.*

Partial penetration
Don't forget that even once you've got to the point where you want to go on to penetrative sex, a little bit of teasing can go a long way! By this I mean through *partial* penetration, and there are a number of ways a man or woman can control this.

Partial penetration techniques for him
While you are on top of your lover, either straddling, sitting astride or kneeling between her legs, you can tease her clitoris with the end of your penis. Hold the shaft of the penis and simply rub it up and down, or use slow, sensuous circular motions. Beginning with her clitoral region, you can then move your strokes down her labia and partially enter her vagina.

In the shower or standing nude or partially clothed, you can nudge the tip of your penis between her legs and over her clitoral region and use a variety of gentle rubbing motions to stimulate and partially enter her.

Partial penetration techniques for her
You can sit astride him and rub your well-lubricated labia up and down the length of his shaft until he's fit to burst.

You should take your time and use gentle pelvic thrusts for another sensation. Or if you are both in the Spoons or other rear-entry positions, you can carefully take hold of the shaft of his penis and rub the tip of the penis up and down your clitoral region, and in and out of your vagina, without allowing full penetration.

For even more erotic pleasure, after the first few strokes of full penetration, either the man or the woman can take control again and return to these partial, teasing techniques. These delaying tactics can be explosive and with a little imagination you'll discover small variations that yield new sensations.

Bondage suggestions

There are many erotic pleasures to be derived from bondage, and part of the fun is that you are indulging in fantasy and role-play (described in more detail in Chapter Eight). Bondage allows you the opportunity to experiment with different roles – being dominant, submissive and also switching between the two. Let's be clear that bondage and dominant/submissive roles are different from sado-masochistic (S & M) practices.

Bondage is a form of fantasy role play in which restraint, control, developing sexual tension, teasing and sometimes giving 'orders' to get a lover to submit to your 'demands' is all just part of a game. Both participants are always in control and can stop any time they choose. In my view, true S & M is about degradation and pain. Once you agree to take part you relinquish control. (However, many practitioners will have their own definitions or perhaps lump such practices all together.)

Sinful Sex is about erotic pleasure and so I'm not going to get into heavy S & M practices here – you'll need a specialist book for that! On the following pages you'll find light bondage and playful S & M techniques that can help you have a sinfully sexy time.

Using restraints in bondage heightens sexual tension. The

restrained person can't do much more than wriggle around trying to get the dominant lover to touch them where they'll feel some relief from this tension. You can get started with partial restraint – either of the hands, arms, feet or legs. Eventually you can build in as many restraints as you desire. In *Further Information* I've listed a few quality bondage sites for your perusal. There's so much trash out there I wanted you to see the best!

Types of restraints
There are many types of restraints you can use. Around the home, you can use silky stockings or tights, a dressing gown sash, or other cord, ribbon for gift-wrapping, and belts – but make sure they're made of soft leather. Adult shops and Internet sites (see *Further Information*) supply a wide range of restraints, including 'bondage sheets' with velcro straps for the ankles and wrists. These have a positive and negative aspect. On the one hand you can play safely – there are no knots to worry that you can't undo. On the downside there is the 'manufactured' feel – some people need the spontaneity of grabbing whatever is handy to bind or be bound with.

Different ways to bind
There are almost as many ways of binding your lover as there are restraints.

Wrist binding
Simply tie your lover's wrists together in front or behind him or her (if you tie them behind, be aware of your lover's comfort). This is very 'vanilla' – or conventional – and non-threatening. A good place to start.

Hands tied separately
Tie your sexual partner's hands separately to the bedstead, or even – if you use long enough sashes – to the legs of a bed or chair.

Ankle strapping
Use straps to tie your lover's ankles together. This gives him the sense that he can't get away from the dastardly and sinful sex you are about to perpetrate on him! Again, the feet may be tied separately to a bedstead or legs of a chair.

Elbow pinning
Using a sash or belt to pin back the elbows is very erotic as it pushes the woman's breasts out, if she's the one being dominated. However, you'll only have a short time before this gets uncomfortable.

Knee binding
When the knees are bound together, it gives an unnaturally tight squeeze to penetration. This is definitely worth trying if you're into experimenting with different sensations.

Exposing the genitals
Many lovers like to get creative so that their bondage play literally puts their genitals on display. So, for example, you drape your lover over the back of a comfy armchair and then tie his or her legs apart with ankles bound to the chair legs. This exposes the genitals for teasing – using oral methods, or sex toys, or both.

Blindfolds, masks and gags
Blindfolding your lover's eyes can heighten her sensitivity to skin sensations. This is because as soon as one sense (sight in this case) is blocked, the others work overtime to compensate. Blindfolds can be used to great effect during innocent touching as in the 'feathering' and 'ice play' mentioned previously. However, when it comes to bondage and domination, blindfolds add an extra edge to your sex play. Some people enjoy wearing masks of different sorts in bondage play. This includes the dominant person, who may decide to hide his face. Obscuring the face or eyes lends an air of mystery – people can engage in the fantasy that they're

being dominated by a stranger. Some people like to play with 'gags', too, but exercise caution if you want to try this. In particular, be very careful that they don't slip and cause choking. **You've been warned!**

Dress for success

You don't have to kit yourself out in head-to-toe bondage gear to get the desired effect. By wearing the traditional colours of domination – black and scarlet – coupled with your highest heels, you'll instantly add to the atmosphere. But it may be worth your while investing in some sexy bondage clothing – anything in leather or PVC, high-heeled boots, black stockings, even a slinky male thong for him. Simply buying one item such as a corset, mini-skirt, basque or, for a man, a genital bondage strap (there are loads of varieties!) can invigorate your sex session.

On the edge – S & M

Many people believe that some pain can enhance the pleasure of sexual activity, hence the saying, 'It hurts so good!' Certainly, pain increases muscle tone, which in turn leaves it ready for further stimulation. Historically, self-flagellation was used to bring people to a state of religious ecstasy and you can see how this might be transformed into sexual ecstasy. In the Middle Ages, when flogging and birching were regularly used as a religious penance, many found the heightened state that was released in them very exciting and pleasurable – and they desired more.

As mentioned, I'm only touching on 'vanilla' S & M, so here are just a few considerations to get you started. Many find the physical and verbal 'accessories' that go with S & M and discipline are stimulating in themselves. Barking some orders at a lover who's playing the part of your sex slave, either restrained or made to kneel at your feet, takes only a little imagination. In this role-play situation you could order your lover to bend over so that you can take her from behind, or tell him to suck and lick you, or kiss your spiky-heeled boots, until you say he can stop. The feeling that giving you pleasure is his only concern plays on the idea of ritual 'humiliation' that we associate with this sort of activity. But remember, this is only a game. You need to agree in advance how far to take the verbal demands.

Spanking and whipping

When it comes to the physical side of S & M, most people think of spanking and whipping. Both practices increase blood flow to the area of skin that is being spanked or whipped, making that person potentially more orgasmic. You can then add some fantasy talk. For example, you may decide it's part of a role play involving a schoolmaster and a young teacher who's just joined the staff and has failed to meet certain standards.

Spanking can be done with the hand or any safe imple-ment you deem suitable – such as a big wooden spoon, the back of a hair brush, or a purpose-made spanking paddle obtained from an adult shop. Some implements have an optional fur-lined side for a gentler spank! As with restraints, whipping can run from the very 'vanilla', such as a dressing-gown sash, to the 'hard-core' using a thin leather whip that is guaranteed to sting and probably draw blood.

A quick smack or slap to the buttocks or thighs delivered during sex (as long as you know your sexual partner will appreciate it) may be as far as your lover is willing to go. Alternatively, pinching – particularly as your lover reaches orgasm – can heighten that pain–pleasure threshold and hint at other erotic pleasures to come. Use these 'vanilla' techniques to get a feel for what the two of you will enjoy.

Always exercise care and common sense. For example, never whip anywhere near the eyes for obvious reasons (although lovers don't always think of the obvious when they're sexually aroused). When spanking, target different areas of skin and don't concentrate on one spot otherwise you can cause bruising or even permanent damage from repeated spankings in the form of broken veins and mottled skin. So vary where you wield that spanking paddle! Any good 'top' worth her salt knows this. A 'top' (or 'dom' – short for dominatrix) is a professional who either dominates or acts sadistically to a client. A 'bottom' (or 'sub' for submissive) is someone who seeks pain, humiliation or both.

Other odds 'n' ends
There are all sorts of nipple/genital clamps and chains you can get to add a little variety. The range of devices available is quite amazing, and they can be applied to all parts of the body. I cover cock rings and anal plugs in Chapter Nine, but suffice to say these also come in quite handy to liven up bondage and/or S & M sessions. And, as mentioned in Chapter Four, handcuffs can be useful too!

Sexual furniture
There are all sorts of items of bondage 'furniture', available from specialist shops, resembling old-fashioned torture racks, stocks and punishment chairs. Some items are for 'stringing up' your lover in order to expose certain pleasure zones such as the delicate perineum and anal area for sex play. These are designed not to cause physical harm (unless used inappropriately).

Water sports
Some sexual partners like the humiliation, or daring, of 'water sports' – that is, urinating on their lover or being urinated on. For the water-sports novice, it is best to experiment in the shower or bath where it causes less mess and seems less threatening. However, for fantasy role-play, I think a good alternative is to pour warm tea slowly over someone's back or stomach, particularly when they're blind-folded. This gives the sensation of warm urine without the 'yuck-factor' experienced by those who don't find actual water sports their 'cup of tea'. Beware, though, of heavy water sports-play involving, for example, urinating into a

tube that has been inserted into your lover's rectum (male or female) or vagina – you can spread STIs and other nasty germs by doing this.

Rules of sinful engagement

To ensure you both derive maximum pleasure from any sinful practices consider the following.

Code words

Agree a neutral word that means you want to stop whatever you're doing. I say 'neutral' because other words that you would normally rely on, such as 'no' or 'stop' may be part of your role play, making it difficult for your lover to distinguish when you really mean them.

No pressure

No one should be under any pressure to engage in these sorts of activities. There's a big difference between suggesting trying new things and talking about a fantasy, and exerting emotional pressure to go through with it. Pressuring or threatening a partner to do something that they find unappealing or humiliating is unacceptable, and not part of a loving relationship. Never play these games with someone you don't know well or don't feel you can trust completely.

Protect airways

Don't play any game that involves restricting a person's airway.

Keep control

Don't get into bondage/S & M games when under the influence of drugs or having consumed more than a small amount of alcohol. Drugs and alcohol can change your pain and inhibition thresholds and lead to mistakes. This, in turn, can be dangerous, depending on the sex games you are playing.

Undo restraints
Never leave anyone alone when they are tied up or restrained. It's not a joke to try to scare them and accidents can happen. (Better still, keep the restraints loose enough for your sexual partner to slip out of unaided. Don't forget – it's only a game!)

Knot practice
It's always a good idea to know how to undo a knot before you tie it. Apart from the obvious risks, it can really detract from the mood if you've tied up your partner and teased them until they can't take any more, and you're both dying to have full sex, and now you can't get them undone!

Take care
Don't do anything that risks injury. If there is a chance of falling, use pillows and cushions to protect you. Avoid using restraints for too long. Bear in mind that, for example, tying your lover's hands behind his back may feel fine at first but gets very uncomfortable later on.

Consider hygiene
When someone is tied up, and you're both getting carried away, it's easy to forget common rules of hygiene. Let's say the restrained lover has asked to be pleasured with a vibrator. She's really enjoying it and in the heat of the moment you begin to anally stimulate her and then return to her genitals. Not a good idea. Any sex toy used in the anal area should be washed before it is used on other parts of the body. A good idea is to keep two sex toys on the go – one for anal pleasure only and the second for genitals and other erogenous zones.

Anal sex
Anal sex has been practised by different cultures throughout the ages. For example, the ancient Sumerians had highly enlightened views about sexual practices and both hetero- and

homosexual anal sex was widely practised. Certainly long before other forms of birth control were available, anal sex gave pleasure without the risk of pregnancy.

Although anal sex is now legal in many Western countries, there is still a taboo associated with it. Many people feel uncomfortable about exploring anal sex and, as always, no one should be pressured into it against their wishes. If you would like to try anal sex, here are some issues to bear in mind in order to make it as pleasurable as possible for both lovers.

 Before you get started, make sure your lover's anal area and your hands are clean. Even if going for straight anal penetration, fumbling around with a condom or latex gloves can mean you may be touching this delicate, potentially germ-laden, area. You don't want to introduce germs either way – from your hands to your lover or from your lover's anal area to you.

 Trim your nails so they don't cause unnecessary discomfort.

 Your partner's rectum needs to be emptied, either naturally or with the help of a suppository purchased from the chemist, and he/she should expel any wind (preferably in the privacy of the bathroom).

 It's incredibly important to be relaxed before penetration commences, particularly for the person being penetrated – if he/she's tense there's no way the anal sphincter will relax. And this is crucial as anal penetration is the exact opposite of what the sphincter and rectum were made for. Foreplay should have got your partner thoroughly aroused before anal sex.

 You may find that, at first, anal penetration is difficult. So agree that you're simply going to indulge in a little anal play to begin with. You may put a condom or latex glove on your finger and try fingering your partner's anus first. Next insert one finger gently but don't move it – just leave it there 'resting' to allow the anal sphincter to relax. Or indulge in a little anilingus – otherwise known as 'rimming' – with a dental dam between your tongue and your partner's anus to prevent transferral of bowel bacteria such as *E. coli*. Or with a condom on your penis, you may gently rub the tip of your penis up and down your partner's anal area and perineum to help him/her relax.

🐍 You'll need to apply loads of water-based lubricant as the anal passage does not lubricate itself in the way the vagina does. Reapply lubrication regularly during anal play.

🐍 For anal play, use extra strong condoms, which will reduce the risk of HIV and other infections.

🐍 You may wish to start from the Spoons position or Doggy style, with your partner well supported by lots of pillows or cushions. Ensuring your partner's comfort will keep him/her relaxed. As you start to penetrate, your partner should also gently (again) try to expel wind, as this temporarily relaxes the sphincter.

🐍 Let the person who is being penetrated control the depth and speed of penetration at first. Damaging the anal sphincter through force can sometimes lead to faecal incontinence, so it is important to have anal sex only with someone you trust.

🐍 To avoid an embarrassing trip to casualty, only use sex toys for anal play that are smooth, unbreakable and flared at the base. Anything else could cause a painful spasm or slip right inside, requiring medical attention.

🐍 Even the most willing partner in receiving anal sex may experience pain or discomfort for a couple of days afterwards.

🐍 Don't forget to warm him up with some 'perineum play'!

🐍 *Sinful Secret... What's good for her is good for him! Anally penetrate him with a sex toy. About 30 per cent of strap-on dildos are sold to straight couples. A man's prostate gland may be stimulated by anal play through pressure on the 'inner wall' of the rectum that can enhance his orgasm!*

Slowing him down

The Taoists believed that there was a special point on a man's perineum where pressure felt particularly erotic and *slowed* his ejaculation. So that makes two benefits – pleasure for him and longer lasting sex for you both! Rub the 'pad' of your thumb on the spot of his perineum that corresponds with the location of his prostate gland – about midway between the base of his testicles and his anus. The rubbing should be in a circular motion – ask him how much pressure he likes. During penetrative sex, if he feels like he's going to ejaculate too quickly, either of you can apply pressure to this spot (depending on what position you're in, one of you may find it easier to reach). This sort of pressure will slow his ejaculation down and doesn't have the negative connotations of the 'squeeze' method. The 'squeeze', when applied wrongly (particularly at a passionate moment), can be very painful and lead to negative feelings.

Pearl Necklaces and other sinful delights

Once you and your partner decide to get more adventurous, there are many other games you can play, such as the Pearl Necklace. This is where the man pulls out of his partner's mouth during oral sex and ejaculates over her neck and décolletage – creating a necklace effect. This is something you might do during bondage sessions or when playing out roles such as the Sex Slave. It can add to the role play and the sense of getting dirty.

Feminising him

Many couples like to try a bit of gender-bending – sometimes involving a little bondage, too. The man may hint at or suggest this, and often his partner feels quite aroused by the idea of feminising him. If this is unexplored territory, you can relax him by turning the game into a fantasy in which you dominate him and 'insist' he allows you to feminise him. Start slowly by putting mascara or lipstick on him before your lovemaking. Or why not spoil each other a little by painting each other's toenails.

Taking it a step further, let him feel your silky knickers by rubbing them up and down his stomach and genitals. Then slip them on him! You may take this sex play as far as you like – he could end up wearing your stockings, suspenders and miniskirt. You could end up in his suit. You might even decide to spend an evening in reversed roles – ending up with a night of passionate lovemaking. But do listen to your partner – and respect how far he's prepared to go.

 Sinful Suggestion . . . Keep that lipstick handy for him to trace around your nipples for an erotic feel and look. Men love exotic looking nipples and before strippers had nipple 'pasties' to glue on they used lipsticks or cosmetic 'tints' to highlight and attract attention to their nipples.

Going knickerless

It's always erotic to feel that you two have a private joke going. One sinful suggestion is for both of you to go out knickerless for the evening. As you both make small talk at a party, no one else will know that neither of you is wearing underwear. Plan to meet up for a quick and naughty grope at some point during the evening. Or when dining at a restaurant, seat yourselves next to each other so you can have a little feel of the other's uncovered genitals. One of you might even like to surprise your partner by innocently announcing over dinner (or wherever) that you don't have any underwear on. Have fun with it!

Flashlight fantasy

A novel bit of fun may be enjoyed by taking a torch to bed with you. This allows you to play 'explorer' under the sheets and examine closely whatever you find! Spread your legs and let your lover explore you – but only if they agree to kiss and lick what they discover.

Try another version of this to create more trust and intimacy between you – this can also be a highly erotic experience. Turn the lights down low and ask your lover to lie back comfortably on some pillows. Spread their legs, sitting between them, and gently massage/touch each little part of their genitals. For example, with your hands well lubricated, you may use fingertip 'fluttering' or 'tapping' (gently!) to trace a line down her inner or outer labia, giving her a wonderful feeling. Or you could use a gentle kneading, circular motion down the shaft of his penis – picture delicately holding it and moving down it. Then continuing with your thumbs around his testicles and down his perineum. All the while you're touching you should whisper how lovely your partner looks. This is sinfully sexy for both of you to experience.

Sinful Suggestion... Devise your own secret sex signature – something you can call your own. It may be a particular type of kissing – possibly somewhere intimate – or the use of an implement for sensual touching. Whatever it is – enjoy it and perfect it!

Don't forget that using some of these sinful suggestions to take your sex play into new territory can be exhilarating. But while you're coming down from your adrenaline buzz remember to show some tenderness! When you're finished with lovemaking always caress, whisper to, cuddle and hold your lover. You'll both come down to earth more gently that way.

8

Sinful Fantasy Play

The human mind is a fantastic sexual playground. It's capable of imagining a vast array of sexual fantasies that have never actually been played out by the person concerned, and probably never will be. This fact doesn't stop our minds from running unfettered down erotic valleys and up sensual mountains, creating our own personal adventures at every turn.

Because of its very nature – taking us to places we're unlikely to visit in reality – fantasy play is a valuable tool in keeping an intimate relationship alive. Most studies of sexual behaviour find that nearly all men and roughly three-quarters of all women own up to fantasising, at least occasionally. Despite this, many people are reluctant to share their fantasy life with their lovers. Usually they fear the other will think they're some sort of sex maniac, will be surprised by the variety of their fantasies, or will feel threatened by them – thinking that the fantasy is preferred to real-life lovemaking.

Fantasy, generally speaking, does serve a purpose. It allows us to escape at least momentarily from perhaps the routine, even dull and boring shape our everyday lives may take, particularly in terms of our sex lives. Many people tell me that the one major downfall is not that they don't love their partner (they do!) but that sex falls into a predictable routine that eventually becomes a rut. In such cases partners often use fantasy to take them out of the soulless sex they're experiencing and allow their minds to race through a selection of erotic situations.

What those who don't share their fantasies fail to realise is that the old saying 'two heads are better than one' is also true with regard to fantasy. By talking about it together, two lovers may start to share the fantasy and then embellish it, making it all the more exciting and arousing.

What do people fantasise about?

In sex surveys, people report having a very wide range of sexual fantasies. Although many of the themes are the same – power, control, surprise, danger, stranger sex, exhibitionism – the way they are played out can vary from one survey to another. I'm going to quote those most often mentioned to me over the last twenty years in my work as an agony aunt, psychologist and life coach, and in my extra research for *Sinful Sex*.

Let's take a peek at the average person's fantasy life. Perhaps 'average' isn't the right word, as no one's average, but I want to convey the more regular, popular fantasies. I'm not going into too much detail, as they'll either tally with one or two you've thought of or stimulate some fresh ideas. Either way, your fantasy life is your own private world and I'm not going to give you 'designer' ones – it's good exercise for your most important sex organ – your mind – to be creative. But first a warning…

Do not misconstrue the human mind's capacity for exploring risqué scenarios as a licence to proceed with real-life scenarios with your partner. No one reading these lists of fantasies should take them as confirmation that, for example, every woman wants to be dominated or every man wants to sleep with a nun. Fantasy, particularly those shared between trusting lovers, may venture into areas the individuals actually have no desire to explore outside of the confines of their relationship and imagination. Don't take this for granted!

Female fantasies
Here are a selection of the fantasies that women have related to me over the years.

Sex with a stranger
This is a popular fantasy with those who long to have a taste of no-strings sex – something society often still regards as a 'no-go' area for women.

Exhibitionism
Many women love fantasising about playing the role of stripper or lap dancer – being the object of male desires and making men go weak at the knees.

Forced to strip
Some women who are inhibited about their bodies relish fantasies in which they're forced to flaunt themselves.

Group sex
Abandoning caution and enjoying the feel of writhing flesh and complete hedonism inspires group-sex fantasies.

Lesbian fantasies
Curiosity about same-sex fantasies is extremely common. If we enjoy close relationships with women we may wonder what they'd be like as lovers.

Being secretly watched/spied upon
Many women simply want to feel desirable. They may have little confidence about the way they look but this fantasy vehicle allows them to play out a positive response to a man spying on them – and being aroused by what he sees.

Sex with the repairman

Or it might be the delivery man, or a doctor, or anyone providing such services to you. These are sexual myths played out in TV and literature, so many women wonder if the repairman can 'fix' more than their washing machine, or the doctor 'treat' more than their health.

Forbidden sex with a friend's partner

Or he could be a sister's boyfriend, or whoever. Fantasy allows us to be as naughty as we'd like. And what could be more sinful then ravishing your best friend's lover?

Exotic sex

This often involves being swept off to a foreign country against your will to be kept as a sex slave. Again, this is a fantasy that allows us to be free of inhibitions and guilt, if only momentarily. Being swept away against our will means that anything that is 'done' to us is not our responsibility – so we can lie back and enjoy it!

Sex with famous people

Sometimes we all need a complete escape, and what could be better than to fantasise that a favourite celebrity wants to have passionate sex with us.

Lady of the manor and the stable lad

This fantasy fulfils two needs. Getting dirty with a 'bit of rough' fuels the desire that many women have of being ravished by rough hands, out of doors. Plus, taking on a dominating role – in this case ordering the stable lad to do your bidding – is a popular theme in women's fantasies. Dominant women can carry their dominant nature into their fantasy lives, and submissive women can let go and change roles.

Giving sexual instruction to a novice

You may be the schoolmistress and your fantasy male an 18-year-old virgin, allowing you to venture into taboo territory.

Domination and bondage, discipline and sadomasochism
Again, experiencing the taboos of domination – in the safety
of your fantasy world – can be extremely erotic. You only
need to think back to the powerful erotic tension in the film
The Piano to understand how handing over power can
become the stuff of fantasies. It was generated by the sexual
demands that Harvey Keitel's character placed on Holly
Hunter's mute pianist character, who eventually yielded
with some passion of her own.

Forced sex
This could involve being taken forcibly or being forced by a
lover to do a new and forbidden sexual practice. As with
being swept out of the country by an exotic stranger, being
forced into sexual acts 'against our will' allows us to play out
completely different roles.

The casting couch
A popular fantasy with many women, in which they have to
give sexual favours in return for a job, money, help, or
whatever. Mixing a 'work' scenario with sex plays out the
theme of power in workplace relationships.

Starring in a porn film
The idea of being the best at sex and so starring in a porn film
arouses many women – who all too frequently think they're
not very good in bed. It also satisfies the need for some
raunchiness when sex seems too predictable and 'clean'.

High-risk sex
This means having sex anywhere there's a chance of
discovery – the 'mile high club', in the office behind the
stationery cupboard, in a lift – you name it. The thrill of sex
where someone may catch you out plays to the desire to get
away with something naughty that lots of women fantasise
about.

Male fantasies

There's a lot of crossover between male and female fantasies. However male fantasies seem to run more frequently into the 'danger zone' than female fantasies.

Sex with forbidden people

Whereas women fantasise about forbidden figures such as schoolmasters, men often take this further and not only fantasise about schoolteachers but ultimate forbidden figures such as nuns and nannies.

Sex with prostitutes

Many men wonder what it'd be like to get their wallet out and pay for sex. This also plays into the realms of getting really dirty during sex.

Inspiring a timid librarian

Being irresistible to women who he thinks are uninterested in sex (unfairly too, as I'm sure librarians enjoy great sex as much as anyone!) allows a man to fantasise that he can seduce anyone.

Being seduced by someone forbidden

Like women, men relish the idea of doing the dirty on their nearest and dearest, such as a best friend's girlfriend – or even mother.

Domination and bondage

Again men are just as curious as women about playing different power roles in fantasy sex play, including discipline and sadomasochism.

Group and three-way sex

Men view group fantasy sex slightly differently from women. Men – and women – often love the sensual idea of seeing and touching many different bodies at once, and men can also fantasise about proving themselves by satisfying a 'crowd'.

Watching lesbian sex
Many men fantasise about watching two women make love together – perhaps believing it'll reveal all sorts of secrets about women. Men also fantasise that they'll be invited to join in!

Watching his lover being taken by another man
The fantasy of seeing your partner having sex with someone else is more common with men than women. It may appeal to some men's competitive instincts, imagining she'll roll over and say, 'You're not as good as my man!'

The businessman and the office staff
This one is about power and abusing it. Being 'bad' and doing the things you'd love to do – lording it over your staff – having them at your sexual beck and call.

Being seduced by a sexy nurse
This fantasy appeals to a man's need to be looked after in *every way*.

Gay sex encounter
Many men are simply curious about sex with another man. But most won't admit it!

Being 'feminised'
Men are so constrained by their social roles that many are aroused by the fantasy of swapping places – their lover putting make-up on them or dressing them in their lingerie.

The officer and the beautiful prisoner
Again a control fantasy – as a policeman or prison officer, the man has total sexual control over someone in his custody. Uniforms and handcuffs add to the erotic nature of this one.

Dirty/raunchy sex with a bag lady
Men are more likely than women to fantasise about having sex with an unwashed street person. It appeals to a man's

earthy side where he doesn't want to be told to smell nice and have fresh breath!

Having sex with a pregnant woman
Some men are fascinated by the idea of a pregnant woman with ripe breasts and a lush stomach.

Seducing a stranger on a train or plane
Being irresistible to a stranger has tremendous appeal to men – who often worry about their desirability. The no-strings aspect of sex with a stranger appeals to men who want sex without commitment.

Super-stud
Again, following the theme of proving themselves, men often fantasise about being the world's greatest lover.

Seducing a younger woman
This fantasy takes the pressure off his lovemaking skills, as he'd be able to instruct her to do his bidding. And in the fantasy she'd see him as an incredible master of sex.

Seducing a gorgeous film star or pin-up
For many men, this fantasy is seductive not only because a film goddess is beautiful but also because it boosts his ego to imagine winning over a woman that other men desire.

Anal sex with a woman
As many women are averse to anal sex, the practice is a bit of a taboo – and that's like showing a red rag to a bull.

Directing or starring in a porn film
Either being a porn star or telling other actors in a sex film what to do gives a man the fantasy of complete control in a sexualised environment.

Successfully sharing your sinful fantasies

Any of the above and many, many more fantasies can be shared with your lover. Simply follow these erotic rules of play:

 As a general rule, put your lover centre stage in the fantasy, particularly if it involves other people. However, there are exceptions, for instance if you are centre stage, as in a lap-dancing fantasy, or your lover's fantasy is watching you having sex with someone else.

 Vary the fantasy themes you share with your partner. Don't keep describing the same scenario or else your lover may think you want to act it out for real, and may feel threatened by this.

 Beware of total honesty when describing fantasies that include people you both know personally. For example, your boyfriend's brother may be gorgeous but sharing that thought with your boyfriend can be intimidating and may cause a row.

 Always ask to hear your lover's fantasies, too. If you have an active imagination it is all too easy to dominate fantasy chat. So play fair, and let your partner have a turn. This will also allow you to savour the new and different scenarios your lover comes up with.

 Fantasies can be wonderful things, but you need to consider the 'turn-off' factor. If you know your partner is repulsed by a particular sexual practice, such as a 'golden shower', keep this fantasy to yourself.

 You may have a sexual partner who simply won't get into fantasy chat and play. Trying to pressure a lover to open up his or her fantasy life may backfire. Instead, try to respect his inhibitions. It may even pay off in the long run. As you build trust within your sexual relationship, you could try occasionally dropping into your bedroom conversation a non-threatening fantasy such as, 'I sometimes fantasise about you wearing those beautiful red silk panties in bed. And that I slowly peel them off of you.' Your lover may come to see that gentle fantasies like this can enrich your sex life.

Taking fantasy to role-play

The wonderful thing about role-playing a fantasy is you can release inhibitions and experiment with hidden aspects of your sexuality. Because you're in a 'role' like an actor playing a part, it gives lovers a sense of freedom to act in sinfully new ways with each other.

If you're just beginning to experiment with fantasy role-play, it is a good idea simply to talk through the fantasy while touching each other and improvising with whatever items of clothing you have at home. In some ways, this is the best form of role-play as it really stretches your imagination. Some people feel truly inhibited when dressing in an actual costume. However, it may be that you can't wait to get down to the fancy-dress hire shop to pick out your Victorian school master's costume or nun's habit. You'll have plenty of selection – these hire shops have everything for a fancy-dress party – just don't tell them it's for your own *private* party!

Adult sex shops also sell a basic range for role-play – French maid, nurse, PVC fantasy clothes, for example. And if you're shy about going into a sex shop, many sites on the Internet sell role-play and fetish clothing.

Role-play scenarios

To get you started, let me give you a few examples of fantasies that translate easily into role-play, without the need for costumes.

Strangers in the night

Agree to meet in a crowded bar. Choose one where you're not known so the regulars won't interrupt your role-play! One of you starts the flirting, pretending you're strangers. Give a fake name and pretend you're married but lonely and in need of some passion. Go to town with suggestive sex talk and erotic touching under the table. One of you will suggest going home and when you get in the door abandon all your inhibitions, as if you've just met.

The boss
For this scenario, you can use a desk, if you have one in your home, or the kitchen table will do. The one playing the 'boss' will sit behind it. The other plays a prospective employee who has arrived for a job interview and is desperately in need of money. The 'boss' describes the job requirements and asks the other to perch on the desk and flash him what extra 'attributes' he or she can offer to the 'position'. Go to town with saucy double entendres! The 'boss' may go as far as they want describing all other 'special' requirements – like having three-way sex with the secretary. The interview culminates with the 'boss' taking the 'job candidate' over the desk for wanton sex.

The randy repairman
All he has to do is put on jeans and a T-shirt and show up pretending he's going to 'fix' something. You sit him down for a cup of tea before he starts the 'job', standing above him flaunting the fact you don't have knickers on while he exclaims about the 'state of the pipes' or the 'tools in his box'. He reaches out to touch you while you tell him how lonely you are. Soon his 'power tool' will be fixing your desires.

Sex slave
One of you pretends to lock the other up as a captive. You are bossy and dominant and order your prisoner to do your bidding. She protests but allows her dress to ride up, 'accidentally' showing her knickers. You describe in vivid detail everything she's going to have to do for you. You can also reverse the roles so that she's the dominant captor – the woman hungry for sex with a hot and horny guy. You have to perform for her – or else!

The sexy maid caught pleasuring herself
She is on the bed playing with her favourite sex toy when you – the master of the house – 'sneaks up' on her. You command her to put on a show with the toy. She protests but

you threaten her with losing her job. You then both become passionately aroused.

I hope these examples show how much can be done with a fantasy role-play without the need to hire special costumes. Remember that simple props you find around the house can be used to add 'reality' to role-plays – just put that imagination to sinful use!

When fantasy can become a problem

A person's fantasy life can become a problem if he or she can *only* gain sexual arousal and climax through 'visiting' the fantasy. In other words, like a sexual fetish where the person must have a fetish 'object' present to achieve sexual satisfaction, the person feels compelled to concentrate all his mental energy on a particular fantasy or he won't experience sexual 'pleasure'. I put 'pleasure' in inverted commas as having a fantasy wield complete control over the ability to achieve sexual enjoyment prevents us from truly enjoying our sexual encounters and other sensual pleasures. A person who is dominated by a fantasy may become detached from the lover he's with – his sexual partner simply becomes a physical vessel in which that person 'gets off' on his fantasy.

But *Sinful Sex* is much more about pleasure and less about sexual problems so I'll say only a few words about this. Prevention is better than cure in such cases. When you fantasise, keep your fantasies varied. At other times, don't 'visit' your fantasy life, instead simply engage mentally with the moment and your lover. Also by discussing your fantasies with your lover, she'll quickly point out if you seem completely focussed on one fantasy to the detriment of your sex life.

Some final words

Fantasy should be used and enjoyed as part of a sinful repertoire of sexual techniques. There'll be times when fantasy chat and role-playing can enliven your sex life and other times when you simply want to focus on the here and now – the touch and smell of your lover's skin, the feel of your partner's lips kissing you, and the sound of their love noises. Flexibility in your approach and communication with your lover will allow you to judge the mood of the situation – and whether or not fantasy play will enhance it.

9

Sinful Toys, Playthings & 'Potions'

Sex toys, catering for all sorts of pleasures, have been around for thousands of years. To mention just a few, the ancient Greeks used dildos made of wood and leather lubricated with olive oil, the Chinese made sex toys from jade and other fine materials, and the Indians used ivory. The late-Edwardians had weird and wonderful electric 'appliances' for use in their lovemaking. Despite the fact that sex toys have such a long and illustrious history, and are big business today, many people still feel a little threatened by them. A man may worry that a woman wants to replace him with a toy, and a woman may feel he's only thinking of kinky sex and not of her needs.

If you'd like to experiment with toys and your lover is a 'toy-virgin', think carefully how you'll introduce one into your lovemaking. Don't stride into the bedroom wielding the biggest vibrator money can buy (and let me tell you, there are some 'big boys' for sale!). Instead, when engaging in sex talk, whisper about a little fantasy of yours. Tell your lover how, in your fantasy, you indulge your partner with exquisite pleasure by gently teasing him (or her) with a sex toy. Gauge your lover's reaction and take it from there.

Because of the huge variety of devices available, I'll give you a 'rude review' of the ones I think most people get pleasure from. So enjoy this. As there is such a wealth of toys on the market to choose from, I'm not going to promote any particular brand, as function, design and 'feel' are such personal decisions. However, you're best advised to make your intimate purchases from reputable adult shops or Internet sites (*see Further Information*) – not some back-alley operation.

Non-powered sex toys
When most people think of sex toys, they automatically think 'vibrator'. Yet there are many toys on the adult market that'll give you sinful sensations but don't require batteries (or mains power – this kind have become popular again, and I do worry about the safety of some of them). So let's begin with these.

Persian love beads
Famous for being worn by ladies without lovers, Persian love beads usually come four to a string and are inserted into the vagina or anus. As the user moves around, so do they – giving pleasurable sensations. Love beads are akin to self-administered foreplay. For those with lovers, as these gentle teasing sensations arouse you you'll soon be thinking about sex with your partner. Some women enjoy the sensation of having love beads inserted anally while their lover penetrates them vaginally. Leave one bead outside the anus – you can then slowly and gently pull the rest out during her orgasm to enhance the experience. When worn anally by men, they can stimulate the prostate and – again – be pulled out gently during orgasm. Make sure you use plenty of lubrication when using the beads anally. Try the new 'soft' pliable beads available for more 'sensitive' people.

Oriental love balls or eggs
Love balls/eggs come in pairs and are made for vaginal insertion. They are slightly larger than love beads but give pretty much the same sort of sensation. It all depends on

your personal preference. They can be sinfully erotic when you have your lover insert them for you – and are less fiddly than the beads. The two of you will know they're in your vagina as you go about your errands for the day.

Anal butt plugs
Originally a gay sex toy, butt plugs can be enjoyed by straight men – and women – too. A butt plug is usually shaped like a mini-lava lamp (if you remember those from the seventies) and holds itself in place in the rectum. Butt plugs need lots of lubrication as the anal passage does not lubricate itself. They come in a range of sizes and can be worn to give sinful sensations before sex, during foreplay, and during penetration (with a woman). There is a range of slimmer, shorter, fatter and 'threaded' ones.

Dildos
A dildo is shaped like a penis, more or less. But, unlike a vibrator, it does not vibrate. Some women and couples prefer these as they can be manipulated by either partner while the other focusses his or her attention elsewhere. And there is no distracting noise – even the noiseless vibrators 'hum'. Dildos are used to stimulate the vagina or anus by being moved in and out and around in circular motions. They can be made from all sorts of materials – and if you're a material girl they can come encrusted with semi-precious materials from upmarket adult shops!

A dildo with a difference
The 'accommodator' is a rather strange-looking toy but with amazing powers to please a woman. This device is worn by a man (or woman in a lesbian relationship). It is strapped to the chin so it can penetrate her vagina while oral sex is performed at the same time – for double the pleasure.

Double-ended dildos
These can be used by lesbians or straight couples in two ways: either to penetrate her vagina and anus at the same

time or to penetrate one of her orifices and his anus at the same time. Sharing a dildo in this way can be a bit tricky, as you might imagine, as you have to shunt your genitals up towards each other. A good way to do this is to sit facing each other and then bring your genitals together. If the man is going to be anally penetrated he can then lie back and twist on his side. She can remain 'seated' or lie back too. Once a double-ended dildo is in you both, you need to gently move together using a rocking motion in order to experience pleasure and keep the two 'heads' of the dildo inside you.

Strap-on dildo

As mentioned in Chapter Seven, it's not only lesbian couples who buy strap-on dildo harnesses. Straight couples do too. Many men enjoy being penetrated by their lovers, allowing them to play out all sorts of fantasies. This is the sort of sex toy you definitely need to mention tactfully so that he doesn't feel threatened. Of course, he may raise the subject himself. By their very nature, strap-ons require practice. Start slowly, with gentle thrusts, and modify the action as you go along until you've got into a steady rhythm. Some strap-ons designed for lesbians include a dildo for the wearer. As she penetrates her lover, she is penetrated at the same time.

Penile shaft 'sleeves'

These soft and highly flexible 'sleeves' can be worn on the finger or the shaft of the penis for extra stimulation of the clitoris, labia and vagina. They come with a variety of ridges and 'knobbles' to experiment with until you find the one you like best. Lubricate them and then pleasure her manually – she'll love the way it feels. Or slide it on the base of your penis for a different sensation during penetration. She may want to use a sleeve over two fingers when manually stimulating you – men love new sensations as much as women. You can also change the feel of a basic vibrator by slipping a 'sleeve' onto it!

Cock rings
Men who've experienced a cock ring say they enjoy the sensation of 'tension' that builds while one is in place. A cock ring keeps the blood that has engorged the penis during an erection from flowing back out. It is worn around the penis and under the testicles, holding the testicles slightly away from the body. Most men report a longer-lasting erection with extra firmness. Try using a flexible cock ring (rather than one made of metal) as it can stretch for easier placement. Add to the experience by having your lover help you put one on. Lightly lubricate it and slide it on the shaft and under the scrotum. The man should make any final adjustments over the testicles so that it feels most comfortable to him. Couples vary in their preferences. Some enjoy the cock ring during manual sex play. Others like it on during intercourse – sometimes removing it before the man climaxes. It can be put on after penetration has started as a means of adding in extra sex play (and slowing things down). There are various attachments available with some cock rings, such as clitoral or G-spot ticklers, or mini-weights to give a pulling sensation to his scrotum. A cock ring should **not** be used for more than twenty minutes. Don't worry if during this time the penis looks darker than normal – it's the effect of the increased blood that has collected.

Labial spreader
This is perfect for the man who likes something highly erotic and different and for the woman who loves being 'exposed' to her lover. The labial spreader has straps that fasten around the woman's upper thighs and little padded 'grips' that hold the outer labia open. She gets to decide how far she is 'spread' by opening and closing her thighs. With her labia spread open her sensations are increased, as is the visual stimulation he gets! This device ensures sinfully delicious oral sex and is great for unusual fantasy-play – such as playing the 'maiden' who's being 'tormented' by an 'evil knight'! There are two other benefits, besides these sinful ones. She doesn't have to hold herself open – and so won't

get in the way of him giving her oral pleasure. And he doesn't have to use his hands to hold her open either – so freeing them to get up to all sorts of mischief!

Chastity belts
If you want to have an added kick to your sex games and fantasies you can buy beautifully made chastity belts from specialist providers. Truly a sex toy with a difference!

> *Sinful Secret... For a sinfully delicious orgasm contract your PC muscle on the downward stroke of you dildo or vibrator. That is, the stroke that pulls it out of or away from your vagina. Doing these contractions will build you to a roaring release!*

Toys that go 'vrrrrooom!'
There are many styles, sizes and colours of vibrators to choose from. You no longer have to rely on the lurid 'orange' plastic variety that dominated the sex-toy market from the seventies onwards. Now there are more natural colours, artistic shapes and even 'futuristic' designs. As well as giving hours of pleasure to lovers, vibrators are ideal for masturbation (even mutual masturbation) and can help women who've had difficulty reaching orgasm to achieve one. Sex therapists frequently recommend vibrators to women and couples to experiment with in a leisurely and relaxed way, allowing them to get to know their own sexual responses.

Fingertip vibrators
Let's start small but perfectly formed. These come in a few variations that are slipped on to his or her finger and used to vibrate around the clitoral region. But don't stop there, as they feel fabulous on the nipples, the perineum and elsewhere too!

Clitoral ticklers

Sometimes attached to regular vibrators or used on their own, these have little attachments for added pleasure. Some have little 'knobbles' of feather-like ticklers for her clitoris.

The Jessica Rabbit or Pearl Rabbit

Rather strange looking, but once you try it you'll probably love it. The main vibrator penetrates the vagina and the little ears of the rabbit vibrate on either side of her clitoris.

Multiple vibrators

There are some mind-boggling vibrators available that have anal, vaginal and clitoral stimulating 'heads' – all on one toy. These are said to yield a complete sexual sensation experience, but some women may find stimulation of all three zones at once overwhelming.

G-spot vibrators

These are shaped with a bend designed to stimulate the 'front' wall of the vagina and so target the elusive G-spot. Some types are on a 'wand' with a vibrator at one end, while others are thicker. Many women swear by these devices and you can arouse him by kneeling on your hands and knees and allowing him to vibrate you from behind.

Clitoral/pubis vibrators

Flat or slightly egg-shaped, these vibrators 'sit' on the pubis/clitoral region and pulsate. They feel fabulous in a teasing sort of way. She'll be ready for penetration after some time spent with this.

'Bullet' style vibrators

These are smaller (and travel easily!) but still feel particularly nice around the clitoral region, and down the labia and perineum. They may also be used for anal play – but remember the hygiene rules!

Harness style vibrators – the 'butterfly'
This is a fantastic device once you have experimented with it and positioned it how she likes it. Strapping on to the thighs, it has a central, flat vibrating area that is positioned over her genitals. It can yield fabulous sensations if he concentrates on her other erogenous zones while this is vibrating.

Harnesses for him
A number of vibrators are held in place with flexible straps and slipped over the penis and testicles. These have attachments for vibrating against her too during penetration. Some are flexible, with little loops that accommodate a vibrating 'bullet' for her. Others have clit-stimulators of varying designs.

Body massagers
There are various wand-type body massagers that can be used for more than just backache! Giving a wide, sweeping coverage, they feel fabulous across the pubic region, down the inner thighs, and across the genitals and the buttocks.

Glow in the dark
For those of you with body-shy lovers who prefer to make love with the lights off, introduce your partner to a glow-in-the-dark vibrator that you won't lose in the sheets.

Warning!
When using a vibrator for anal pleasure – even if using one specifically designed to be inserted into the anus – make sure you don't let go and 'lose it'. Believe me, from talking to hospital doctors I know, they can travel far into the colon and continue to vibrate, necessitating a trip to the hospital.

Sinful Suggestion . . . Some vibrators are specifically designed for use during penetrative sex in order to stimulate both of you. But ordinary vibrators can also be slipped between you and held there for added pleasure.

Don't forget that sex-toy hygiene is crucial. Always wash them after use, following the manufacturer's instructions. This usually means cleaning the toy in warm, soapy water. For safer sex, cover a sex toy with a condom before inserting it into any part of the body. As mentioned in Chapter Seven, keep anal toys separate from vaginal toys. And keep *your* toys separate from *your lover's* toys! You can use different coloured bags so you can tell them apart. Choose water-based lubricants that won't damage the surface of plastic sex toys.

 Sinful Suggestion... Don't forget to share those good vibrations! Some men are too shy to say they'd like to feel your vibrator between their legs. So, take the lead and give him a buzz by running the vibrator down and around his genitals and over his perineum. If he likes anal stimulation, use a separate toy.

Suspended harnesses

For those with a little extra money to spend, there are some great ceiling-mounted harnesses to try. The harness has comfortable, multiple straps and is designed to suspend your lover over you – either for penetrative sex or fantastic oral sex. With a touch of the hand you can turn her – or him – to allow you a different access point. Very comfortable for him, hugely exciting for her, and risqué for both. You must follow the instructions carefully so that the harness doesn't get pulled out of the ceiling. Another version is the Thai Basket, also suspended above a bed or floor, which your partner sits in. The basket doesn't have any 'weave' in the centre of the seat so there's access to her vagina and anus.

Private pole dancing

For a private thrill, more couples are erecting poles in their bed or 'play' rooms. You can practise your pole dancing and then flaunt yourself to your lover. Indulge in a fantasy where you are a pole dancer and he's a customer who can't resist 'joining' you on stage to fondle and touch you – even though it's against the club rules!

Aphrodisiacs

Like sex toys, aphrodisiacs have a long history. In ancient Mexico, the Aztec emperor Montezuma drank 50 cups of pure chocolate a day to fuel his exploits with his 600-strong harem. The reputed 'love shake' consumed by Cleopatra consisted of ground almonds, spices, honey and yoghurt. Some aphrodisiacs have a basis in fact but others hold a promise that may be more psychological than actual. Here are a selection to consider trying, if not for their aphrodisiac properties then for their ability to seduce you through your senses of sight and taste:

Almonds

These are said to contain properties that can revive flagging desire. In Mediterranean cultures almonds are traditionally regarded as a symbol of love and fertility and are baked into savouries and desserts.

Asparagus

Greens are good for you, and handfeeding your lover an asparagus spear dripping with warm butter is a sensual experience in itself.

Avena sativa

This is often used in preparations with other aphrodisiacs, and seems to boost their effects. Research supports the view that it boosts libido, particularly in people with low testosterone. It is often found in extract form and can be added to food and drinks.

Bananas

Many people love bananas. They're good for your health and said to have energy-giving properties. It's actually an alkaloid in the skin that has the actual 'aphrodisiac' effect so cook them whole. They're great to share, baked with honey, cinnamon, and hot cream – why not spoon-feed each other?

Chocolate

This contains the chemical phenyl ethylamine, which stimulates the brain, boosts energy and gives a euphoric effect. Chocolate often contains caffeine, too, so it can be energising and mood enhancing. Remember how Casanova used chocolate 'love tokens' to romance potential lovers? Something as simple as feeding your lover strawberries dipped in warm chocolate can really raise the temperature!

Damania

One of the most popular aphrodisiacs, its botanical name – *Turnera diffusa aphrodisiaca* – declaims its properties. Grown in hot countries, it is said to create a mild euphoria. Mexican women traditionally serve hot drinks made from damania before lovemaking. It contains several alkaloids that boost the circulation, thus aiding sexual arousal. Sold in capsule form or as a tincture, it should be taken a couple of hours before lovemaking commences.

Ginger, cinnamon and ginseng powder

The Chinese have used ginger as a stimulant for 3,000 years and other eastern cultures use ginseng and cinnamon for the same reason. They can be baked into delicacies or sprinkled into salad dressings.

Gingko biloba

Well known to increase blood and oxygen flow, gingko biloba is said to enhance mood and so aid lovemaking. The gingko tree was originally found only in Japan and China, but is now cultivated in the USA.

Muira puama

Derived from the roots and bark of an Amazonian tree, this extract is particularly popular in Germany. Available in its raw form, you can prepare a brew with it and add it to your favourite drink. It's also available in capsule form and may be mixed with other aphrodisiacs.

Orgasm creams

There are various topical creams (which you rub onto the genitalia) that purport to increase sexual arousal and blood flow to the genitals. Many of them are mild skin irritants – such as the menthol-type products – that simply inflame the skin giving a sensation some find pleasant and others find irritating. Others contain L-Arginine, an amino acid known to increase blood flow to the genitals for about ten to thirty minutes with each application. Always purchase these from a reputable source and read the instructions carefully.

Oysters and other seafood

Oysters contain high levels of zinc, which is beneficial to health and energy levels and vital for fertility. But any seafood can be highly seductive, simply through the way it is presented and its taste.

Padma '28'

This herbal extract from Tibet has undergone clinical trials and been found to be effective in improving blood flow to constricted arteries. Enhancing blood flow is important for achieving arousal.

Scents

As mentioned in Chapter Four, essential oils can play an important part in creating the right mood. Cleopatra (again!) seduced Mark Anthony with rose-scented carpets. Ancient Egyptians used many other fragrances in baths and oils, including cinnamon, jasmine, patchouli, musk and frankincense. The Romans scented every part of their beds, walls and baths, while the Greeks were known to use floral and wine-scented oils on their bodies to heighten their sensuality.

Vanilla
This has been used in various love potions for centuries. It tastes and smells deliciously sensual and is great in scented candles, oils and as a flavouring for a rich dessert to savour.

Ylang-ylang
As well as its beautiful scent, this essential oil is renowned for its euphoric and mildly relaxing qualities.

Yohimbine
This is derived from the bark of the yohimbe tree and evidently is pretty good at increasing male libido. Yohimbine is widely used as an aphrodisiac in Africa and the West Indies. Scientific trials on rodents and humans have shown a positive effect from this product. It boosts neurotransmitter levels and can be brewed into a tea from its natural form or taken as a tincture available from health food stores.

A note of caution
As with any herbal 'remedies', check with your doctor that it is all right for you to use them, especially if you are taking prescription medication. Some herbal extracts can interact with prescribed drugs. Always stick to the recommended dose on any items bought in health or sex shops. Overdosing on yohimbine, for example, in your eagerness to enjoy this aphrodisiac, can cause nausea and vomiting – not sexy!

Medical/Prescription 'Aphrodisiacs'
With over one in ten men aged over 21 experiencing erectile dysfunction at some point in their lives and up to 40% of women experiencing loss of sexual desire at least some of the time, there's a big market for prescriptions to help the sexual response along. These are the most common prescriptions you'll come across:

Viagra
Acts locally by blocking certain enzymes involved in the
erectile process, preventing nitric oxide from breaking down
too quickly. Nitric oxide has vasodilator effects and is
necessary to maintaining an erection. Work is currently
being done on female Viagra and appropriate dosage levels.

Cialis (due to be licensed in Britain in late 2002)
Described as the 'son of Viagra', it works in the same way as
Viagra and may lead to a larger window of time for sexual
activity to take place.

Uprima
This acts by stimulating dopamine receptors in the brain. A
nerve impulse is then produced and transmitted down the
spinal cord via the pelvic nerves, which causes penile
arteries to enlarge allowing the spongy tissue in the penis to
fill with blood.

Alprostadil
Alprostadil forms the basis of penile injections and pellets
(inserted into the urethra) to promote erections.

Testosterone
This product comes in different strengths (male and female)
and as a patch, gel, or cream, and works to boost desire in
men and women.

Phentolamine
A vasodilator helping women's genitals to become engorged
with blood. It is still being researched for its effects but the
US product Vasomax has had promising results.

'Aphrodisiacs' to avoid
Various animal-based aphrodisiacs have had scorn heaped
on them by scientists. In Oriental cultures, there's the belief
that eating the penises of certain animals will give you their

sexual strength. However, the tissue found in those parts is not unlike that in the rest of an animal. Don't buy in to claims – and hefty prices – that potions based on substances such as rhino horn will enhance your virility. These have no basis in fact – rhino horn has about as much aphrodisiac effect as chewing your own fingernails!

Everyone has heard of Spanish Fly, but what you don't often hear is that it can be downright harmful and should be avoided. It is made from ground-up Cantharis beetles. Rather than making you feel sexy, it actually irritates the urinary tract, making you itch. Evidently it can be fatal to some people – so definitely don't try it.

So there you have sinful ideas for toys, playthings and 'potions' to add to your lovemaking. Toys and aphrodisiacs make ideal presents for your lover, helping to keep things lively between you. When buying an erotic gift, try to choose something with your lover specifically in mind. This is a perfect way to show them what they really mean to you – as well as how sexy you think they are. As we move on to Chapter Ten – Sinful Sex Games and Scenarios – you may find some of these toys come in handy.

10

Sinful Sex Games &

Scenarios

People take sex too seriously sometimes – they simply don't enjoy enough fun and games! There's nothing wrong with laughing during sex, when the mood takes you. It's the laughing *together* that's important, rather than laughing *at* your lover. In this chapter, I want to bring more humour into your sexual relationship, by suggesting some sinful sex games and scenarios you can try. Hopefully, once you've tried some of these playful ideas you'll come up with your own versions!

There are all sorts of adult board games you can buy – but why invest money when you can invent games of your own using a little imagination? Unfortunately, too many people feel embarrassed about playing sex games/scenarios or think they'll look stupid, and so they miss out on the potential for erotic fun. For that reason, I'll be happy if you try one of these just *once* in your lovemaking.

Before you start, you may need to go out and do some 'daft' things together as a couple, to put you in the mood for sex games. For example, you could go to a park and let go of your inhibitions by playing on the swings and slides. Or you could visit a funfair and act like teens again. Buy bags of your favourite sweets and rent a silly video to laugh through.

You may wonder how this fits in with a sex guide. Believe me, the more connected you two are when it comes to 'letting go' together, the sexier you'll feel. If you enjoyed some of the suggestions in Chapter Seven, such as bondage play, those are essentially sex games! Any fantasy role-play you enjoyed in Chapter Eight would be regarded by many as sex games too – so these should have given you confidence to experiment further.

Once you feel freer together, sex games will seem completely nonthreatening. That said, you may have a lover who simply can't let himself go and mess around playing sex games. Or a partner who thinks they're tacky and a big turn-off. That's fine – the ethos of *Sinful Sex* is 'each to his own'! I'm simply providing you with some fuel for your fire – it's up to you whether and how you use it.

Sex games people play
The following are simple to try, on the whole, and will stretch you creatively a little while setting a steamy scene for sex to follow.

Truth or Dare
This is based on the game we all played in our youth. You cosy up together with some soft music and sexy lighting, and take turns to tell the truth or take a dare. Begin with each of you writing out five 'dares' on separate pieces of paper. Fold the pieces and place them in a bowl. 'Dares' can be anything you want – trying something new like 'anal rimming' (don't forget the dental dams or cling film), or a bit naughty such as peeing in front of the other, stripping to music, or letting your partner play 'flashlight' on your genitals. The dares, of course, may be so pleasurable or naughty that you'd rather do them anyway!

Now take turns asking each other naughty questions, such as, 'What's the sexiest fantasy you've ever had?' or 'Where's the most unusual place you've ever had sex?' If you don't want to answer you dip into the pot and select a dare. Very juvenile – but, as long as you don't own up to anything that would upset your lover – great fun too.

Porn Star

If you have a camcorder or a Polaroid camera you could set up a fantasy game in which one of you is the director and the other a budding porn star. Your 'porn star' can start playing to the camera but as the director you are so impressed with the performance that you join in. After filming, relax and enjoy the show! For your peace of mind, erase the videos or destroy the photos afterwards, as they've been known to resurface in embarrassing places after relationships break up.

Control Yourself!

Another game is to see which one of you can keep under control during sex. As you two get worked up in foreplay you agree the limits. For example, once penetration starts, he's only allowed five thrusts and then has to withdraw. Or you may be given oral sex but can only receive three little sucks before your lover pauses. Obviously, the point is to find out who can control themselves best. The 'better' lover wins! A great little game for building sexual stamina.

Wish List

You both think of three sexual things you've always wanted to try and then write them down on separate pieces of paper. These are folded, marked with your initials to identify them, and mixed up. You then take turns to draw out one of the other's 'wishes', agreeing in advance to at least give it a try.

Strip Poker

This is a classic where the loser bares all and the winner sees all. If you're not poker fans, you can do this with any card game of your choice. You could even try strip chess, strip Monopoly, whatever. No cheating – make sure you both know the rules! Once one of you is stripped off entirely the lovemaking begins.

Forfeit

This may sound a bit silly but it is a sexy game if you're in a playful mood. One of you has to correctly guess what the other is 'miming' and pay a forfeit if you get it wrong. For example, she may appear to be miming oral sex but she's actually miming sucking his finger. If he doesn't guess correctly he has to pay a forfeit – such as removing an item of clothing, or performing a sex act that only pleasures her – forfeiting his own needs. This is a game you can initiate spontaneously, perhaps when you're cuddled up with a glass of wine and simply enjoying some closeness – it can really turn up the heat!

Sexy Dice

You can buy lovers' dice from an adult shop. Instead of having dots on each side, like conventional dice, these show the name of an erogenous zone that has to be kissed, nibbled, sucked and so on. But it is just as easy to use ordinary dice. The first die will list the parts of the body. Decide between yourselves what the numbers will represent. For example, one is 'breasts', two is 'genitals', three is 'bottom', and so on. The second die represents an action or activity. For example, one is 'a lick', two is 'a thrust', three is 'a rub'. Take turns to cast the dice. The two numbers will give you the erogenous zone and the activity to perform for your lover, such as 'lick' your partner's 'nipples'.

Strangers in the Night

This is based on the fantasy I recommended in Chapter Eight. This becomes a game when one lover decides the plot and the other plays along. This takes some ingenuity but it is great if you two are planning on spending some quality time together and are prepared to indulge each other's whims. One of you – the 'stranger'– selects a fantasy to be acted out. It can be anything along the lines of strangers meeting by accident. For example, you could meet as strangers in a lift, or in front of a shop. The other has to follow the stranger's lead.

After role-playing some flirting with you, the 'stranger' might insist that you have *al fresco* sex in a wood, or that you go to a restaurant and fondle each other under the table. On another occasion you could take the lead, unless submissive sex gets you aroused and you want the 'stranger' to surprise you and lead you astray every time.

Knock, Knock

This is a variation on Strangers in the Night. One of you knocks on the door and pretends to be a visitor with a purpose, such as a police officer looking for a criminal, a plumber wanting to mend a leak, or a nosey neighbour who is investigating a strange noise. Once inside, you start flirting and getting suggestive. The 'policeman' might say he's got some handcuffs that need 'testing'. The 'nosey neighbour' might comment how they 'never knew how sexy you were'. Or you might show the 'plumber' where the pipes are, at the same time bending and stretching so that he gets an eyeful. He may even lift up your skirt and fondle you, exclaiming, 'What a gorgeous body you've got!' You get the message. The suggestive remarks set the scene for playing out a naughty fantasy as a game and the looking and touching lead to sinful sex.

Twister

This is the old-fashioned game, but played with a 'twist'. In this game you two dress scantily and sexily before starting Twister. As you twist into the different positions on the Twister board, you take turns to do 'sinful' things to each other. For example, when it's your turn you reach out and caress an erogenous zone or plant a naughty kiss some-where. Eventually you'll collapse into a heap (as people do with Twister!), ready to get into more usual sexual positions.

Sex Slave

This is another game to play when you have time to indulge each other. You both have to carry out silly tasks to decide who's the 'sex slave'. For example, you have to try to balance a sex toy, such as a vibrator, on your pubic bone. The one who can balance the device longest wins – the other becomes the sex slave. Once the slave is selected the 'master' can indulge any whim (within reason of course!) for the duration. Pre-agree how long the loser will have to be a 'slave' for. One hour? All night? It's up to you!

The Sex Slave Massage
This is a refinement of the Sex Slave game – a tempting 'treat' that the master might ask for. When you give a Sex Slave Massage, remember that you're at your master's (or mistress's) bidding. Dim the lights and cover the master with comfy towels to keep him snug. Using sensual oils warmed between your hands, start on large body areas – the back, chest, abdomen, thighs – then work in towards the more sensitive areas. Vary the touches, building up from fingertips to feathers, to silky sashes, to kitchen brushes, to a vibrator, and back to hands – whatever he asks for or you know he'll love. The master should be made to feel he can relish each moment and demand further touching where he desires. By the end of this you might decide to be a *naughty* slave, having touched your master to the point of no return and then refusing him his sexual release. That'll lead to more fun and games!

I'm Dessert Tonight!
This is an oral sex game. Write out instructions on separate pages of a notepad covering all types of tongue and lip 'action'. For example, a page each for 'lick', 'suck', 'nibble', 'blow', 'flick', and so on. You can toss a coin to decide who's 'dessert' and who's 'eating'! Then select all your favourite foods from the fridge – perhaps you have a sweet tooth that needs *indulging* and you go for whipped cream and chocolate sauce, and maybe throw in some chopped nuts for good measure. Illuminate the kitchen with subtle candle-light and place cushions on the *kitchen table* for padding, covering them with a sheet (for easy clean-up). Your lover has to lie back on the table and allow you to create a dessert

incorporating her (or his) erogenous zones – particularly the genitals! You select three of the instructions and then eat every morsel off her.

Sinful Surprise!
Together, designate a date a week or two ahead. You both have the task of going out and finding/buying something interesting for your sex life by that date. It doesn't have to be a new and unique commercial sex toy (but it could be) – try to be more inventive than that. Originality and thought dictate the winner, who gets to choose which of the two things you try at the appointed date when you unwrap them.

I Spy
Not the traditional 'I Spy' – this is the saucy 'I Spy'. Taking turns, you have to make your lover guess what you have seen. Creativity is the key. You could say, 'I spy with my little eye, something beginning with "a",' and your lover immediately says something sinful like 'ass', but you're actually thinking of the 'areola' around your nipple. This may get you both laughing as you can use all the rude and saucy slang names for genitalia that you know and keep your lover guessing.

What Is It?
Your partner is lying down blindfolded. You lubricate different parts of your body – fingers, toes, chin, tip of the nose, genitals, and so on. You then touch her (or him) in various places. Your blindfolded partner has to guess what you are touching her with! If she guesses correctly, she gets to ask for whichever touch she liked most to be repeated. If she guessed wrong you swap places.

Now you have some simple ideas at your fingertips for making each other laugh and feeling a bit naughty and sexy. So lose your inhibitions and get playing those sinful sex games. It'll add another dimension to your lovemaking.

11

Sinful Solutions to Agony Questions

Everyone worries about sex at some point in their lives, no matter how experienced or adventurous they are. If not worry, you may wonder about your sexual abilities and/or relationship. Niggling doubts are common – such as how you compare with others, are your little kinks 'normal', are you pleasing your lover, how do you introduce a favourite technique to someone new, the list is endless. It never ceases to amaze me how people come up with novel questions or angles for the same old problems.

It would require a whole book to cover all these countless problems and worries, so I'm just going to take you through the 26 questions I'm asked most often as an agony aunt and psychologist. Why are these the most common questions? Because the largest number of people wonder about them! Now that you've read the rest of *Sinful Sex*, you may find a lot of your questions have already been answered, particularly those about your own sexual response, how to communicate, trying new techniques and stimulating some creativity in your lovemaking. If your particular worry or problem isn't mentioned, I apologise in advance for leaving it out. So here goes.

**It doesn't seem to bother my lover when we argue –
he can carry on with sex as usual. Why does it affect
my sexual feelings?**

Men find it much easier to detach their feelings (including
angry ones after an argument) from their sexual desire. But
for most women sex is deeply connected to their emotional
self – so if they're angry or hurt this will block their desire or
arousal. Try to resolve disagreements rather than ignoring
them and allowing them to fester. Be honest and tell him that
arguments have a knock-on effect regarding your sexual
feelings, rather than just giving him the cold shoulder – as
too many women do.

 **I'm five months pregnant, healthy and feel sexy but
my partner seems to have gone off the idea of sex –
what's going on?**

Men often have unfounded fears about damaging the
growing baby. Allay any such worries by showing him a
book on pregnancy. This will give him the reassurance he
needs that it is perfectly safe for a healthy pregnant woman
to have sex. Or you could get him to come to one of your
antenatal appointments, where his questions can be
answered. Men sometimes start to see their pregnant
partners as a mother and – at least temporarily – no longer a
lover. Gentle coaxing, along the lines that you're still a horny
woman, will encourage him to see you in *all* your roles. To
help this, don't drone on too much about the little niggles of
pregnancy – save those conversations for girlfriends!

 **I sometimes retch when giving my partner oral sex –
how can I prevent this?**

Hygiene is very important, so ensure he's always nice and
'tasty' before you start. It can make a woman gag if he tastes
'stale'. It may be that you sometimes take him too far back
into your mouth, setting off your gag reflex. So take care not
to do this accidentally. Keep your hand at the base of his
shaft so your mouth can't slip down farther than is
comfortable.

How does exercise help your sex life?

Exercise is great for your general health, which in turn affects your sexual desire. When we exercise, the brain releases endorphins – natural 'feel good' chemicals. These circulate in the blood and reach every part of the body, including the genital and pelvic areas. Think of exercise as natural Viagra – but don't overdo it, as that can have the opposite effect. Check out the Sex-ercises in Chapter Two. You can do the 'Kegels' during sex; as you squeeze you'll enhance the sensation.

 We were once so passionate, so why is our sex life going downhill fast after two years?

Nearly everyone goes through the 'honeymoon' phase at the start of a relationship where they can't keep their hands off each other. It's the excitement of new, unexplored territory that keeps you wanting more. This builds as you learn to press each other's buttons and give total sexual pleasure every time. But once you've passed through these two phases you often don't know where to go from there. Where once it was so easy to feel completely aroused by your partner, you now feel that you've lost the spark. You just need to find the sexual creativity you have within you (that *Sinful Sex* will have unleashed). This new phase takes a little more effort but, if successfully negotiated, can yield far greater intimacy and passionate sex.

 My lover is very body-shy – how can I convince her I love every part of her?

Her 'body insecurity' has formed over a lifetime and is a very hard habit to break. Be patient. Encourage her by slowly increasing the lighting when you make love. For example, you could start with a couple of candles to cast a little subdued light – building up to a half-dozen or so over a couple weeks. Then, encourage her to flash the part of her she's most proud of – perhaps her thighs or waist. As she sees your delighted response her confidence will grow –

with time! You can also encourage some fantasy play where she's the 'temptress' and you're at her beck and call. Being in control may help her throw caution (and bodily inhibitions) to the wind.

 I'd love to dominate my boyfriend, tie him up and really humiliate him, how can I broach this?

First, always question where this urge to humiliate comes from – does he humiliate you and so it's payback time? If so, this is something you both need to talk over before it gets out of hand. If it is simply a fantasy you wish to play out, dirty talk is a great way to start. Allow it to stray into a little playful talk about humiliation and gauge his reaction. Then get out some soft silky stockings to tie him up with (check out Chapter Seven for more information) and start slowly. Keep it playful – don't make it too humiliating, at least until you know how he will react.

 Why do I lack sexual desire when I have a perfectly nice lover?

There are three main areas that both men and women need to address if they lack desire. First, your lifestyle can affect your desire – for example, if you're stressed, overtired, smoking or drinking too much, or using recreational drugs. Second, if you're depressed or suffering from anxiety, or some other psychological problem, or emotionally troubled by your relationship, your sexual feelings will be greatly reduced. Third, an undiagnosed condition or the medication you're taking for a diagnosed illness can affect desire too, so it's important to speak to your doctor. Examining all of these areas and tackling any issues one at a time should help restore your sexual feelings.

 I'd love to watch my lover masturbate but I don't think he will do it in front of me – how can I persuade him?

The best way to get him to masturbate in front of you is to suggest some mutual masturbation, so that you're both putting your private sex life on view. Expecting him to do it alone is hardly fair. It might be fun to broach the subject while you're lathering each other in the shower. Ask him to show you how he holds and strokes himself when he's on his own. You could promise to let him give you a Pearl Necklace (see page 125) if he'll masturbate for you.

 My lover and I have a fantastic sex life but he still masturbates – why aren't I enough for him?

As noted in Chapter One, 98 per cent of men masturbate (and most women too). Sometimes when men have an active sex life they masturbate more (or at least at the same rate) because they get aroused thinking of the great sex they've just had with you! So don't worry about it, just so long as it doesn't get to the point where his masturbating leaves him no energy for you.

 I'm heading for the menopause and have heard it may affect my sexual desire – is this true?

Many women experience a decline in their sexual feelings before, during or after the menopause, owing to the many hormone changes. These may affect desire and also vaginal lubrication. Talk to your doctor or other health care provider about the options available and use loads of extra lubricant. Look at it as a new phase in your life that can be fantastic. Talk about fears with your lover and start to experiment. Some women find they feel much more liberated at this point, especially as they no longer have to worry about the risk of unwanted pregnancies – you can be one of them!

 Our sex life seems more like hard work than pleasure – why is this?

This usually happens when a couple get into a sexual rut – doing the same thing over and over again – say, Doggy style on a Sunday morning. Even if you feel desire initially, this can soon get damped down by the complete lack of spontaneity. Suggest to your partner that you build in one sexual surprise a month (or fortnight), taking turns to dream them up. (You'll find a wealth of ideas in the preceding chapters!) Hopefully, you'll both soon find that a little imaginative 'effort' takes the 'work' out of sex.

I regularly fantasise about my boss, who I actually don't like very much. Why is this?

Human fantasy life is amazing! We fantasise about all sorts of things we would never actually do. Sometimes fantasies are mixed up with issues of control–power or love–hate feelings, or simple curiosity of the 'what would this be like?' variety. You may experience a sense of power over your boss when you have this fantasy. Or quite enjoy the control he exercises over you. Don't worry – it's just a fantasy to be enjoyed privately by you.

I sometimes fake orgasm – does this matter?

The best, most sinful sex is built on honesty, so orgasms should never be faked. You're not a sex machine and no matter how turned on you are, or how much you care for your lover, your body doesn't always fully respond. With honesty you can say, 'Darling I'm enjoying being pleasured by you and would love it if you orgasm, but I'm not going to get there this time.' This doesn't have to reflect on either of you as lovers, but instead reflects on the honesty and respect you've built up in the relationship.

My wife has a much higher sex drive – isn't it supposed to be the other way around?

That's a great sexual myth – that men are forever horny and women have 'headaches'. Often men settle more quickly into a contented routine where they expect sex on, say, a Saturday night. They are content in the relationship and simply enjoy some regular (and probably not too inventive) sex. Women, on the other hand, want to feel that things are 'special'. They're less happy with routine sex, and often worry that sex is a barometer of the relationship (which it can be). Whenever a couple have a mismatched libido they should aim to reach a compromise. Try varying where and when you have sex to break the routine. If that's successful, but the frequency of sex is still an issue, agree a plan where every other night (or afternoon, or morning!) you take turns to be the 'chooser', deciding whether or not to have sex. The other attempts to go along with the desire of the 'chooser'. If goodwill is shown by both parties, a compromise can be reached.

 My lover is very unhappy about his premature ejaculation but is too embarrassed to go to the doctor – what can I do?

To help him, you need to be a bit of a 'love detective'. Find out if he climaxes rapidly through masturbation, too. If he does, then it may simply be a habit he's got into. If he's slower on his own then the problem may be nerves or excitement at being with you. If so, make love when you're not under time pressure and encourage leisurely foreplay where he concentrates on your sensations rather than his own. Get him to try the exercises in Chapter Two to build self-control and the ability to identify his point of no return. He may find that a combination of masturbating on his own and trying the exercises can help him learn to prolong sex with you. Don't forget that, having climaxed once, he'll be slower the second time around.

 I can't get an erection with my lover at all – what can I try?

First, you need to determine if this problem is 'situational' – that is, can you get an erection when masturbating? Or do you wake up with one in the morning? If not, this may indicate a physical problem that may need medical attention, so talk to your doctor. If you do get an erection at these times, it may be your emotional state that is to blame – perhaps nerves or relationship issues are causing this. Think through the three sets of possibilities that affect erections, as mentioned in the question concerning sexual desire on page 166 – lifestyle issues such as stress or excess drinking, psychological conditions such as depression, and medical problems. These should be discussed with your doctor.

 I'd love to climax at the same time as my lover but it never happens – this really disappoints me.

Don't be disappointed. It's actually quite rare for lovers to climax simultaneously. You're buying into a sexual myth – that the best lovers climax together. The best sex comes from enjoying the moment of orgasm when it arises for each of you. This is only a problem if there's a huge time difference between you and it is causing tension in the relationship (for example, if he suffers from premature ejaculation – see page 169 – or you find it very difficult to reach orgasm – see page 171). If one or the other of you wishes to prolong or hasten your orgasm so that you climax together that's fine – just so long as it's done in the spirit of 'fooling around' and not a goal that must be met.

I'm only 8cm (3in) when erect and don't seem to fulfil my lover's sexual needs – what can be done?

As I've said earlier, if you feel that you are under-endowed, become the 'king of foreplay' – this will more than make up for it. Bear in mind that it is the first 8cm (3in) inside a woman's vagina that has the most nerve endings, so you have ample to stimulate this area. Choose positions where 'tension' is greatest between your two pelvic regions, such as the CAT (see page 58), and allow her to grind into you. You may consider introducing sex toys to give her some deep vaginal stimulation – if she likes that. And you can give her some sinfully delicious oral sex at the same time. If you are still concerned about the size of your penis, you could consult a doctor who specialises in male genitourinary medicine for advice.

It's six months since our baby was born and I still don't feel very sexy – is this abnormal?

Because of sleep disturbance, the demands of a new baby,

the changing adult relationship, and hormonal changes, a woman may find she does not resume 'normal' (for her) sexual activity until between six and twelve months after the birth. Mothers can feel 'babied out' having held, cuddled and fussed their infant all day long, and they may not want to be touched by their partner in the evening. Rekindling affection and romance is the key. Ban baby talk in the evening and just focus on the two of you. Make 'dates' (ideally once a week) with each other where even if you don't want to spend money, you get out for a romantic walk or a picnic. Start with cuddling and caressing, banning sex until you both feel like it – which can come sooner than you think! However, if your lack of sexual desire is part of a wider problem, such as chronic fatigue, lethargy or depression, you should talk to your doctor who may recommend a course of treatment.

 I find it difficult to orgasm with my husband even though I climax when I masturbate – why is this?

As explained in Chapter One, many women have difficulty reaching an orgasm during lovemaking. Since you masturbate successfully (an excellent starting point!) you need to learn to share with your lover the sort of stimulation that makes orgasm possible for you. Consider mutual masturbation, allowing him to see how you stimulate yourself. Look at Chapter Three, for ways to approach this subject with your partner, and Chapter Five, for positions such as the CAT that enhance stimulation during lovemaking. Through masturbation, you know that all's well 'down there' so now it's simply a question of relaxing with him and indulging yourself until you both climax during sex.

 My lover hates PVC, which is unfortunate, as I love the feel of it squeezing my skin tightly. How can I compromise with him?

The best compromise is to introduce just a little PVC, rather than overwhelm him with a whole outfit. Go for a bra or hot pants combined with something you know he likes. That way he'll see you're trying to satisfy both your needs. Ask him if there's something new and exciting that he'd like to try in return for giving PVC a chance.

 I worry about the amount of porn I watch and feel terribly guilty afterwards. My girlfriend doesn't know I watch it.

Secrets have a way of making us feel guilty. It sounds like porn has become a habit that controls you rather than an occasional 'event' that you choose to enjoy. Cold turkey is the best way to break the habit. Get rid of your porn stash and live one day at a time. Each day, remind yourself you only have that day to resist the urge to buy some more. When you think about it, substitute something positive. When you are with your girlfriend, enjoy her and her body. Reserve fantasy to talking with her about scenarios, rather than something secret in your head – which may also lead to guilt. Eventually, it won't have a hold over you and your guilt will diminish, but see a counsellor if it doesn't.

 I've always been with men but lately find myself fantasising about a very attractive woman I work with – could I be bisexual?

You'd be surprised how many men and women have same-sex fantasies. This may be a matter of simple curiosity or a sign of deeper feelings. Human sexuality is not set in stone and is much more fluid than many people realise. If you're single and would like to check out these feelings then feel free. You'll soon find out whether you wish to keep them as fantasy only or take them further.

 When should I have sex in my new relationship?

There are two main goalposts for knowing when sex is 'right'. First, when you feel you can *talk* about it. Too many people with little confidence find they have slipped into bed before they can discuss their desires and needs. If you can't talk to your lover you shouldn't be having sex. Second, when you feel *in control* of the timing then the time is right. If you're feeling under pressure, either from your lover or from some notion that you 'should have sex *now*' then you're not actually in control. The best lovers are those who have the confidence to control the timing of sex.

I'd love to spank my lover but worry about her reaction – how can I fulfil this desire?

In Chapter Seven, I describe how important it is to bring up subjects like this tactfully – often as part of sexy, fantasy chat. Whisper seductively about this desire to her and then, if she seems responsive, ask, 'How's this?' as you tap her bottom *gently*. You'll soon gauge what she thinks of this idea, but without upsetting her. To make it even more interesting, tell her you want to play fair and let her spank you. Don't invest in a spanking paddle until you know what she feels.

 Sinful Secret... Try 'trading places' with any sex problem you have. Ask your lover to step into your shoes and see how it feels. Then take the liberty of role-playing your partner. Both of you may then be in a better position to make suggestions that might work with the hurdle you face.

Now we've come to the end of *Sinful Sex*. I hope it's been a pleasurable journey of uninhibited discovery for you. Remember, we all experience our sexuality in a unique way. Learning to share your desires and needs with a lover, discovering theirs, and bridging any differences is a wonderful part of developing real intimacy. I hope by now you're comfortable with your own body, you understand what brings you sinful and delicious pleasure, and are confident about being creative with a lover. Allow yourself to continue to explore your sexuality and you will enrich your relationships – and your life!

Happy loving.

Further Information

Useful numbers
British Pregnancy Advisory Service – 08457 304030.
Family Planning Association helpline – 0845 310 1334.
The Gender Trust, for help with gender issues – 07000 790 347.
Institute of Psychosexual Medicine, for help with issues of
    sexuality and gender – 020 7580 0631.
Relate couples and relationship helpline – 0845 130 4016.
Sex Addicts Anonymous Information – 020 8946 2436.

Sinful Websites!
You may find these websites helpful in choosing sex toys,
    erotica, and getting information!
www.goodvibes.com A fantastic all-round US shopping
    experience.
www.condomania.co.uk For all your condom needs.
www.amandakiss.co.uk Adult toys for girls and boys.
www.blissbox.com Sex toys for women – that men will also
    enjoy.
www.sh-womenstore.com Don't worry, many of the toys
    and outfits available here are for both of you!
www.Myla.com Sells sex toys and lingerie for discerning
    tastes.
www.annsummers.com The 'popular' end of the sex toy

and lingerie market. Try **www.annsummersuncut.co.uk** for more hard-core products.

www.blushingbuyer.co.uk For shopping without embarrassment. Products for all your personal needs.

www.skintwo.com For your fetish wear needs.

www.eroticprints.org The Erotic Print Society for erotica of all types.

www.cliterati.co.uk Erotica for women.

www.erotica-readers.com For your erotica and creative needs.

www.scarletmagazine.co.uk A sex and erotica magazine just for women.

www.mr-s-leather-fetters.com A top bondage site based in the US.

www.fetters-leather.com A top British bondage site.

www.fetteredpleasures.com The website for the North London bondage shop.

www.agentprovocateur.com Gorgeous and sexy things for women.

www.coco-de-mer.co.uk The luxury adult shop.

www.wickedlywildwomen.com A site for women.

www.adameve.com An inventive site for men and women with wonderful toys.

www.impotence.org.uk For impartial advice about male impotence.

The Seven Sexy Sins

- Secretly explore your own body so you know what excites you.

- Seductively tell your lover what you love.

- Sexily ask your lover what you can do for them.

- Scintillate your lover with tales of your secret fantasy life.

- Sensuously indulge your desire for new positions.

- Spontaneously take your lover somewhere new.

- Sinfully continue to experiment from time to time.